MAKING OFFERS THEY CAN'T REFUSE:

The Twenty-One Sales in a Sale

Third Edition

by

Stan A. Lindsay, Ph.D., Teaching Professor

Florida State University
at Panama City, Florida

Spring 2015

Say Press
Orlando, FL

Library of Congress Control Number
ISBN: 978-0-9914793-1-3

TABLE OF CONTENTS

PART THREE: AUDIENCE = PROSPECT

PART FOUR: AUDIENCE = DECISION-MAKER

PART FIVE: AUDIENCE = CLIENT

To **Larry and Wanda Fritz**

My Siblings-in-Law

Whom I Haven't YET Had the Joy Of Meeting

and

Andrew Lindsay

My Dad

INTRODUCTION

Sales Theory

Sales is nothing more than *persuasion with the implication that the exchange of money is involved*. The **actual exchange of money** is usually taken to be the evidence that the attempt at persuasion has been successful. While it is true that sales *implies* the exchange of money, the actual act of persuasion in which the money is exchanged represents only one of the **twenty-one acts of persuasion** that are typically involved in the making of a single "sale."

Fortunately for those who would be salespersons, the various means by which humans are persuaded have been taught by some of the greatest thinkers in human history. Chronologically listed, some of these thinkers are: Socrates, Plato, Aristotle, Jesus, and St. Augustine, as well as some important late-comers--Kenneth Burke, Richard Weaver, and Stephen Toulmin. Long before I was actively involved in sales, I was a student of these thinkers. In 1979, the year I began my sales career, I completed the last of my coursework for a Ph.D. in Rhetoric at the University of Illinois.

When the **ancient Greeks** first began to formulate the art of persuasion (or rhetoric), the primary use of the art was **to *help* individuals**. **Democracy** was new. In the past, individuals who were charged with a crime had been simply at the mercy of the ruling tyrant. Now, with Greek democracy, someone who was charged with a crime had the opportunity to provide a defense in court. The art of persuasion was formulated to enable the accused to persuade the court that the person charged was innocent. Aristotle called this use of persuasion **judicial rhetoric**. In judicial rhetoric, the persuader attempts to persuade a judge or jury concerning the nature of something that **occurred in the *past***. The goal of the persuader is to persuade the audience that the accused is either *guilty* or *innocent*.

Since democracy dictated that issues of the city-state would be determined by deliberation and debate, those who could persuade others in the assembly could **help to direct the government**. The goal was **to determine the course of action that would be most *expedient* for the city-state in the *future***. The art of persuasion was used to help the society at large. Aristotle named this use of persuasion **deliberative rhetoric**. In this text, deliberative rhetoric will be the primary focus, since **business proposals** are designed to recommend *future* actions. The clear **purpose of a business proposal** is *to determine and recommend the course of action that would be most expedient for the business entity or client.*

While it is true that there have always been those who have used the art of persuasion selfishly, the great minds of the discipline have always belonged to individuals who sought to help others. When the art of persuasion has been abused, leaders of the discipline have severely criticized the offenders. Plato called those who abused the art of persuasion **"sophists."** It was these sophists who, in Plato's estimation, gave a bad connotation to the term rhetoric. To this day, the term "sophistry," according to *Webster's*, denotes "deceptively subtle reasoning or argumentation." Many people still use the term "rhetoric" in a pejorative sense. Jesus called those who attempted to persuade deceptively "hypocrites."

Plato, Socrates, and Richard Weaver

I had studied the writings of **Plato,** who, according to Schiappa (1992), coined the term **rhetoric** to designate the *knack of persuading human beings*.[1] Plato presents his teacher, **Socrates**, as one who does not have much appreciation for those who have the knack for persuading others.   Plato thinks that it is easy to use this "knack" of rhetoric **unethically**, if persuaders use their "knack" to persuade audiences *that what is actually false is the truth*.   Plato, therefore, would consider salespersons unethical, if they attempt to *mislead* their prospects into believing that false statements made in the sales presentation are actually true.   **Richard Weaver** (1953), an advocate of Plato's teaching, agrees.   He defines rhetoric as **"truth plus its artful presentation"** (p. 15).   Socrates and Plato, as philosophers, believed that they could arrive at *truth* by the use of what Plato's student, **Aristotle**, would later call "*logos*" (or logic).   But, while his student Aristotle did not necessarily agree with him, Plato thought that *truth* was something each human possessed, down deep inside of himself or herself.   He believed that this *truth* was something that each human soul originally possessed in an **ideal world** that exists and something that each human soul had experienced, before that human was born into the physical world. Therefore, Plato and his teacher Socrates were accustomed to using **Socratic questions**. Instead of trying to **argue** for a specific position on an issue, the Socratic (questioning) method simply asked questions, and then, based on the *logic implicit in the answers* their audience gave to the questions, they would *ask follow-up arguments*, until their *audience arrived at truth through the audience's own reasoning*.   While **Platonism** (Plato's philosophy), with its presumption of an earlier ideal world existence, seems to many scholars a difficult concept to accept, it was, at least, an attempt to explain where certain intangible concepts originate for humans—something that might be called *an intuitive feeling about the immanent nature of reality*.   According to Weaver (1953), there is a level of knowledge that is "an intuitive feeling about the immanent nature of reality."   Weaver calls it **the "metaphysical dream"** (p. 30-31).   It is difficult to locate tangible evidence, for example, of concepts such as *justice* and *freedom*, yet it is clear that humans hold such *intuitive feelings* to be *real*.   Perhaps, even the idea of *ethics*, that causes Plato and Socrates to resist rhetoric's tendency to prove that the false is true is one of those *intuitive feelings*.   Sales and other forms of persuasion must take into account such *intuitive feelings*.   Later in this book, as the concept of selling one's own credibility is discussed, we will discover an example of something that seems *logical*, but is plagued by *intuitive feelings* that it is somehow *unethical* or *inappropriate*:   the fact that humans intuitively feel negative about an individual expressing his or her own credentials.   We call it "tooting one's own horn" or "bragging."   Why do we have this

---

[1]See Plato (1973), 89 and Plato (1971), 43-47.

ethical dilemma about giving others our credentials? Why are we embarrassed that we are "patting ourselves on the back"? Is some intuitive feeling at work?

Plato (1968, bk. 7) taught his concept of the process of finding true reality by telling a story. We may term the story a "**myth**" or a "**parable**," but it helps us visualize the way Plato sees the learning process of humans. As a salesperson, you might view yourself as the one in Plato's story who helps others to "see the light." Plato describes the scene: several humans are chained in pitch darkness in the inner sanctums of a cave. They see very little "light" (a metaphor for knowledge). Their backs are toward the slight, flickering light that trickles in from the mouth of the cave. The only "knowledge" these chained humans believe they possess is in the faint shadows they see flickering on the wall of the cave. Gradually, one solitary individual breaks the chains that have imprisoned him in darkness and begins to crawl very slowly toward the distant mouth of the cave. This is the individual's process of learning—his quest for true knowledge (that Plato and Socrates believe was always a faint flickering light in the soul of the individual). A song that puts Plato's **Parable of the Cave** to music has the following lyrics:

Plato's Cave

(Words and Music by Stan A. Lindsay)

- The story you're about to hear was written long ago. The author was the Greek philosopher, Plato. The setting is the deep, dark, down recesses of a cave. The dim, refracted light within is knowledge that can save. Some men have been chained all their lives, their faces toward the wall. They see their own few shadows flickering so small. To them, the truth is nothing but the shadows that they find. They do not know the shadows come from light that lies behind.

- Light! Light! Learning is the light. It can shatter every speck of darkness in the night. Even blinded beggars, as they learn, regain their sight. If the light means knowledge, learning is the light.

- Suddenly, a single man begins to break his chains. The bonds upon the other prisoners remain. And, as he slowly turns around, his eyes are filled with pain. His eyes have not adjusted. The dim light makes him strain. And, slowly, he starts crawling toward the source of all the light. Every inch along, he's suffering; he fights. The pain grows with the brightness every step along the way. And then he loses consciousness. He sees the light of day.

- Light! Light! Learning is the light. It can shatter every speck of darkness in the night. Even blinded beggars, as they learn, regain their sight. If the light means knowledge, learning is the light.

- Finally, he awakes because his eyes, at last, can stand to see the trees, the grass, the mountains of this land. The man is overwhelmed by all the beauty of this sight. He's thankful for that painful day he fought his way to light. He now remembers the others and decides just what to do. None would believe him though he swore it was true. And, as he led them out in pain, he knew that they would fight. And yet, it would be worth it all, if they could see the light.

- Light! Light! Learning is the light. It can shatter every speck of darkness in the night. Even blinded beggars, as they learn, regain their sight. If the light means knowledge, learning is the light.

Aristotle

While Plato coined the term rhetoric, but was always somewhat suspicious of those who practiced the persuasive arts, his student **Aristotle** not only appreciated those who could persuade, he **wrote a book on the subject**, *The Rhetoric*, which still remains, more than two millennia later, the standard work on persuasion in the world. If you would learn how to persuade, you should turn for guidance to Aristotle.

Aristotle (1991) **defines rhetoric** as "*an ability in each [particular] case, to see the available means of persuasion*" (p.36). He then proceeds to identify the **major "means" of persuasion**. Beyond what Aristotle calls **"inartistic proofs"** (i.e., evidence that is not created by the persuader, such as laws, witnesses, contracts, etc.), Aristotle suggests that there are three primary means of persuasion (**artistic proofs**). These are *ethos, pathos,* and *logos.* In this chapter, I briefly consider each of these means, but first I make a distinction that is key to the **ethics of selling**. The distinction I make is that which exists between **coercion and persuasion**.

Coercion vs. Persuasion

A complaint that is sometimes registered by a purchaser who has subsequently experienced "buyer's remorse" is that the salesperson "forced" or "pressured" the buyer into purchasing. "Pressure" and "force" are not identical, however.

"**Pressure**" is that which produces "**stress.**" I discuss stress more fully in my book, *The seven C's of stress* (2004). There, I claim that there are seven basic sources of stress: *corporal, cash, community, chrono, competence, conscientious,* and *confusion.*

"**Corporal Stress**" is any stress that is generated **by the body**. If someone is tired or ill or in pain, s/he feels stress or pressure. Yet *this* pressure is generated by the prospect's body, not by you, the salesperson.

"**Cash Stress**" is any stress that is produced by the necessity of performing **money management**. Clearly, this is a stress that is common to the sales encounter. If the prospect wishes to purchase something, but does not have sufficient money, there may be *cash stress.* You do not force the prospect to buy, and *unless there is a true desire on the part of the prospect* to buy, there is *no* cash stress. Furthermore, even if there is a desire to buy, no cash stress exists unless there is an *insufficient money supply.* You do not produce this situation. However, if you persuade the prospect that the product is desirable, the cash stress may develop naturally. You can frequently *relieve some cash stress* by showing the prospect *ways of saving enough money* elsewhere to make this purchase feasible. In **Sale Number Sixteen**, I discuss the ways in which **feasibility** is sold.

"**Community Stress**" is the stress that is felt when two or more humans, wishing to cooperate with one another, differ in their individual goals, tastes, values, wishes, etc. Since your goals and tastes often differ from those of your prospects, you need to be resourceful in overcoming this stress. In **Sale Number Eight**, **Eleven**, **Twenty**, and **Twenty-One**, I offer advice on alleviating this stress.

"**Chrono-Stress**" is stress caused by the perceived need to accomplish something within a **fixed time limit**. This is often the type of stress which prospects have in mind when they accuse you pressuring them. Frankly, this is often a necessary pressure in the sales process. Without the commitment on the part of the prospect to make a decision within a fixed time period, you, as a commissioned salesperson, become an **unpaid teacher**. You will experience *your own version of chrono-stress*. You may not have enough time to see the number of prospects necessary in order to make a livable income unless you ask the prospect to become a decision-maker before conducting a complete sales interview. This issue is discussed in **Sale Number Thirteen**.

"**Competence Stress**" is the stress one feels when one **questions one's own competence** to perform a task (such as making a decision). This stress may be due to a *lack of self-esteem*, a *lack of knowledge* on the subject, or a *lack of "negotiation/purchasing" skill*, etc. To relieve this stress, you need to be a **good teacher**. If the teaching is thorough, the prospect should know everything necessary to make an informed, competent decision by the end of the sales interview. The prospect should understand the evidence that *a problem exists*, the main *cause(s) of the problem*, the available *solutions*, the *efficacy* of those solutions, and the *feasibility* of those solutions. I discuss these issues in **Sale Number One**, **Two**, **Ten**, **Fourteen**, **Fifteen**, **Sixteen**, and **Seventeen**.

"**Conscientious Stress**" is the **moral stress**. Whenever there is a "Thou Shalt Not" combined with the inclination to violate this "Thou Shalt Not," there is conscientious stress. Sometimes (as in the example of selling life insurance), the best **moral course** is to purchase the product for the protection of one's family. The "**immoral**" inclination is to selfishly refuse to protect one's family. Here, your objective may actually be to provide some pressure (i.e., conscientious stress).

The seventh and final stress is **"Confusion Stress**." This occurs whenever **someone feels lost.** If this stress occurs, it is possible that the salesperson is either *inept* or is an out-and-out *charlatan*. To create this stress is frequently *the objective of carnival shysters*. To intentionally produce confusion stress in a sales interview is *immoral*. It is a purposeful attempt to have the prospect make an uninformed decision.

My purpose in discussing **these stresses/pressures** is to demonstrate that while various pressures may exist in a sales context, their existence does **not necessarily indicate that the salesperson has violated any moral codes**. Indeed, you as a salesperson might be less than moral if you do not encourage some stresses. Yet, frequently, you are able to *reduce* many stresses or pressures that arise naturally.

Force

None of these stresses, however, indicate the use of force or coercion. Coercion usually involves the employment of physical force. At the very least, it involves the *threat* of physical force. I present a fuller explanation of my distinction between coercion and persuasion in my book, *Implicit rhetoric* (1998a, p. 5-7). For present purposes, I will summarize.

There are **two principles of coercion**. We use these two principles whenever we train animals. They are the "*pleasure principle*" and the "*pain principle*."

My neighbor once installed an invisible fence around his yard. It consisted of an underground wire circuit that transmitted a signal to the area within one or two feet of the wire. His dogs wore receivers on their collars. Whenever one of his dogs approached the wire too closely, the signal from the wire activated an electric shock mechanism in the collar of the dog. This is the **"pain principle"** at work. The dogs were trained by *stimulus and response* that certain areas on the fringe of their yard were painful. Hence they stayed within the parameters preferred by their owner. This is *coercion*. We use coercion on animals because **animals** (since they do not use language) **are incapable of being persuaded.**

The "**pleasure principle**" is also used to coerce. If a cat comes whenever the owner calls, "Here, Kitty," it is probably responding to the "pleasure principle." The cat associates the sound "Here, Kitty" with the pleasure of being fed or petted. This is also *coercion*.

Persuasion

Persuasion, on the other hand is the *use of nothing but words and other symbols to produce a desired action on the part of some person.* In *Implicit rhetoric* (1998a), I have a chapter (p.145-160) entitled, "Prayer as proto-rhetoric." There, I point out that in some systems, theoretically, **gods** are persons who **cannot be coerced**. In these systems, one does not typically think of forcing God to do anything. However, some people believe that *God may be "persuaded."* Many assume that by **praying**, they can motivate God to do what they want him to do. The *use of words and other symbols* are the only means by which they believe they may motivate a god. Thus, prayer is sometimes viewed as **pure persuasion**.

Animals can only be coerced. *Gods* might only be persuaded. **Humans**, of course, *may be either coerced or persuaded*. **War** is the attempt by humans to *coerce* certain behavior on the part of other humans. **Spanking** is the attempt by parents to *coerce* certain behavior on the part of their children. **Giving pleasurable rewards** (candy, ice cream, cookies, etc.) is also the attempt by parents to *coerce* their children. It can be argued that some humans are coerced to work at jobs they don't enjoy by the pleasure principle of the paycheck just as slaves were coerced to work at jobs they didn't enjoy by the pain principle. But, **in sales** (as in other forms of persuasion), **we do not try to coerce**. We *use only words and other symbols* in order to persuade our prospects to choose a certain course of action. The prospect has the **free will to choose** either to purchase or not to purchase. There is *no force*. **If the exchange of money is the result of force or coercion, we call it robbery, not sales.**

The Means of Persuasion

Now that we understand that sales is persuasion, let's consider the **three basic (artistic) means of persuasion** taught by Aristotle: *ethos*, *pathos*, and *logos*.

Ethos

The English word **ethics** comes from the word *ethos*. **Ethos** means *credibility or trustworthiness.* The **very first means** by which we are persuaded, is *ethos*. We learn to trust the word of our parents. I often ask my university students to indicate by a show of hands how many of them at one time in their lives believed in the existence of Santa Claus. Statistically, the result is usually between 90 percent and 100 percent. I then comment on how ridiculous this belief is. How can a fat man work his way down countless chimneys, most of which are far narrower than he? Many houses do not even have chimneys. How can he fly through the air in a sleigh pulled by reindeer? How can he manage to make all of these toys? How can he transport and deliver all of these presents within a single evening? I ask my students *WHY they believed such nonsense*. Their answer: Their *parents told them* it was true.

I turn to those who did not believe in Santa Claus. *How could they not believe* in something in which 90 percent or more of their friends believed? Their answer: Their *parents told them* it was not true.

Ethos is the **first means by which humans are persuaded**--we simply trust the word of certain individuals. Back to the Santa Claus example. The child who believes is soon confronted with a **crisis of *ethos***. Someone at school (usually, his name is Billy) tells the believer that anyone who believes in Santa is stupid. Billy goes through the litany of objections to Santa's existence that I mention above.

The child now confronts his/her mother, "Mom, Billy says there's no Santa Claus!"

The mother reassures, "Well, Billy's wrong. There *is* a Santa Claus." The child must now determine which source has more *ethos*.

16

The child returns to school. "Billy, you're wrong. There is *too* a Santa Claus. My mom said so!"

What is it about some individuals that makes them more trustworthy than others? There are essentially **two elements in** *ethos*.

The *first element* is "**expertise**." Children naturally trust the expertise of their parents in their early years. When they are two years of age, they ask countless questions. They simply assume that their parents know all of the answers. Their peers, however, are another matter. Their peers are asking the same questions they are. How could a child assume that a peer would know as much as a parent?

The *second element* is "**active goodwill**." The child instinctively asks him/herself: Does the person to whom I am speaking possess a large amount of goodwill toward me? I know that my mom loves me--she tells me so. Clearly, Billy has less goodwill for me than does Mom. So, when faced with a crisis of *ethos*, I choose to trust the word of my mom more than the word of Billy.

Car repair shops sometimes have a bad reputation. I personally have taken my car to shops to obtain a cost estimate for a repair. Sometimes I have been told that a problem would cost hundreds of dollars to fix, only to discover later that the repair could be made for a few dollars. The offending shops do not have "active goodwill" toward me. I usually have my car repaired by a friend or family member who does care about me personally. However, there have been times that my friend or family member was not sufficiently knowledgeable about a particular problem and how to repair it. In dealing with repair shops who have expertise but do not have goodwill toward me and in dealing with friends or family members who have goodwill but insufficient expertise, I have paid at times for repairs that were not needed or that were not correctly completed. The best solution to my car problem is to find a "friend" who possesses "expertise." Both of these elements are necessary for someone to possess strong *ethos*.

Salespersons typically face difficulties with establishing *ethos*. They are often not well-known to their prospects. Furthermore, since salespersons earn commissions, many prospects assume that sales types do not have "active goodwill" for their prospects, and are only concerned with making money. In **Sale Number Three**, **Eight**, **Eleven**, **Twenty**, and **Twenty-One**, I discuss ways in which we may establish *ethos* successfully.

Pathos

From the Greek word *pathos* come such English words as sym*pathy*, em*pathy*, a*pathy*, and anti*pathy*. The "-pathy" element **means "emotion**," as does the term *pathos*.

"**Sympathy**" adds the element "sym," which means the same as the English word "sum" (the total resulting from mathematical addition). So, "sympathy" *means adding your emotion to someone else's* emotion. For example, if my friend's dog dies, I express sympathy: "I'm sorry to hear that your dog died. Although I didn't know your dog, I know that he was very special to you. I know that you are feeling bad and that makes me feel bad."

"**Empathy**" adds the element "em," which means the same as the English word "in." "Empathy" denotes the situation in which *two people have the same emotion in both*. Returning to the example of the death of the dog, I might empathically comment: "I'm sorry to hear that your dog died. I remember theday my dog died. I was in my house when I heard the screeching tires, the dull thud, and my dog's yelping. I ran as quickly as I could. She died in my arms. I know just how you feel."

"**Apathy**" adds the element "a," which means the "absence" of something. Atheism means the absence of a god/*theos*. "Apathy" means the *absence of emotion*. If I have "apathy," I might comment to the grief-stricken pet owner: "Your dog died? Get over it! There are plenty of dogs in the world. Go to the pound! Get another one and quit complaining!"

"**Antipathy**" adds the "anti" element which means *to be "against"* someone or something. If I hold "antipathy" towards someone whose dog has died, I might say: "Your dog died? Good! I hope your cat dies! I hope your car dies on your way to work! I don't like you!"

A salesperson certainly should **not** have *antipathy* toward the prospect, and if a prospect feels antipathy toward the salesperson, there is little chance of a sale. *Apathy*, while it is certainly better than antipathy, is not desirable either. If salesperson and prospect develop a sense of *sympathy* or, even better, *empathy, a good deal of persuasion* is possible. Aristotle suggests that emotions are powerful means of persuasion:

- anger,
- love,
- fear,
- shame,
- goodwill,
- pity,
- confidence,
- kindliness,
- envy,
- emulation,
- enmity,
- friendship,
- shamelessness,
- being indignant, and
- shame

Only if one **loves** one's spouse and children will one be inclined to purchase life insurance. If one **pities** the poor, one might be persuaded to give to charities. If one is **angry** at drunk drivers, one might join MADD. If one **fears** dangerous individuals in one's city, one might buy a gun. If one has **enmity** towards one's college rival, one might buy competitive T-shirts, etc. If one **envies** rich people, one might be inclined to vote against them when they run for office. If one, on the other hand, feels **emulation** toward rich people, one might buy their financial help books and recordings. If one feels **friendship**, one might buy a gift for someone. If one feels enough **shame**, one might buy an *even more expensive* gift than one had planned. If one lacks **confidence**, one might buy esteem enhancement products. Emotion is persuasive.

Logos

The English word "logic" comes from *logos*, the final (artistic) means of persuasion which Aristotle offers. Reasoning or **logic is of two varieties**--*inductive reasoning* and *deductive reasoning*.

Inductive

When we use **inductive reasoning** (reason "inductively"), we begin with the assumption that "nothing" is known in advance. We then begin to compile **examples** and try to draw **conclusions from our examples.** For example, if I see a stalk of corn that is fully mature, I might notice that its height is about 7 feet. I might draw the conclusion that a mature stalk of corn stands 7 feet high. If I then look at several varieties of corn, I may find that mature stalks range in height from 3 feet to 8 feet. The more examples that I consider, the more valid my conclusions may be.

Statistics comprise a part of inductive reasoning. If I notice that 75 percent of the students in my university classes typically wear denim as a part of their clothing, I might *conclude* that "denim is an acceptable fabric choice for college student clothing." If I observe that fifty-one percent of automobile accident fatalities involve alcohol, marijuana, or cocaine use, I may *conclude* that there is something in alcohol and drugs that contributes to automobile accident fatalities.

Deductive

While *inductive reasoning* begins with the **assumption** that *nothing is known in advance*, **"deductive reasoning"** begins with the **assumption** that *at least two things are known in advance.* The two *things that must be known* are called **"premises."** The **"syllogism"** is the *basis of deductive reasoning.* In a syllogism, there are **three elements**—a *major premise*, a *minor premise*, and a *conclusion.* Plato attributes the *discovery of the syllogism* to *Socrates.* Here is Socrates' handiest example of a syllogism:

Major Premise: All humans are mortal. *Broad statement of fact*

Minor Premise: Socrates is a human.

Conclusion: Therefore, Socrates is mortal.

20

The **major premise** is usually a *general statement of fact*. The **minor premise** is usually a *specific statement*. Trying a more contemporary illustration, we might propose the following:

Major Premise: When the President of the United States enters at an event, "Hail to the Chief" is played.

Minor Premise: Barack Obama is President of the United States.

What would be the conclusion? Of course, it would be:

Conclusion: When the Barack Obama enters at an event, "Hail to the Chief" is played..

We may also use inductive reasoning in conjunction with deductive reasoning. The result is called an "enthymeme." It looks like a syllogism, but is based only upon "probable" truth:

Major Premise: People do not want to die. (Deductive)

Minor Premise: Fifty-one percent of automobile accident fatalities involve alcohol, marijuana, or cocaine use. (Inductive)

Conclusion: Therefore, people "probably" should avoid alcohol and other drug use when driving.

Stephen Toulmin

Contemporary philosopher **Stephen Toulmin** (1964) builds upon the syllogism (p. 94-145). He suggests that the three elements of the syllogism are not enough. He offers **six elements**. His *first three elements*--data, warrant, and claim--are *similar to the three parts of the syllogism*. "**Warrant**" is like "Major Premise." "**Data**" is like "Minor Premise." "**Claim**" is like the "Conclusion." I will illustrate Toulmin's system using the most famous legal case in recent history--the O. J. Simpson trial(s).

A "**warrant**" might be stated as a *general piece of knowledge*: "Blood found at a murder scene which is not the blood of the victim(s) is the blood of the murderer."

The prosecution produced *examples* and *statistics* (inductive reasoning) to demonstrate the following piece of "**data**": "O. J.'s blood was found at the murder scene."

Then, the prosecution made a "**claim**": "O. J. murdered Nicole and Ron."

21

This looks very much like a syllogism or, at least, an enthymeme. However, Toulmin does not allow us to stop here. He provides three more elements--*rebuttal*, *backing*, and *qualifier*. The six elements of the Toulminian system may be remembered using the following mnemonic device: **"Washington, D.C. RBQ."** Think of going on a trip to Washington, stopping at an Arby's restaurant, and ordering an Arby-Que sandwich.

- **W**ashington stands for warrant;
- **D** stands for data;
- **C** stands for claim;
- **R** stands for rebuttal;
- **B** stands for backing;
- **Q** stands for qualifier;

A **rebuttal** may be offered *against any data, warrant, claim, or backing*. It usually *begins* with the word *"unless."* For example, we may offer a **rebuttal against the claim** that "O. J. murdered Ron and Nicole," *even if we allow the data and warrant to stand*. We may say: **"unless** O. J. was also a victim." This rebuttal was not used, but it could have been tried.

Taking another stab at it (pardon the pun), we may **rebut the warrant**. We may agree that blood found at the murder scene that is not the blood of the victim(s) is the blood of the murderer **"unless** it was not murder at all, but self-defense." Again, this rebuttal was not used. We may also **rebut the warrant** with the words, **"unless** the blood was *planted* by a racist police officer." This rebuttal was used in the actual case.

Thirdly, we may attempt to **rebut the data**. We may say that O. J.'s blood was found at the murder scene **"unless** the DNA evidence is faulty" or **"unless** it is the blood of that other one person in a billion who has the same DNA code." These rebuttals were also used by the Simpson attorneys.

Backing is the *answering of a rebuttal*. It usually *starts* with the word *"but."* For example, if the rebuttals, "unless it was self-defense" or "unless O. J. was also a victim," had been tried, a

backing might be: "**But**, O. J. never admitted to being in the vicinity of the crime." A **backing** to the rebuttal, "unless the blood was planted by a racist police officer (i.e., Mark Fuhrman)" was: "**but** Mark Fuhrman did not have the opportunity to plant the blood."

To this latest *backing*, a **rebuttal** was tried: "**unless** a large number of police officers conspired to assist Fuhrman." The **backing** to this rebuttal could be: "**But** there is no evidence that the other police officers were racist or that they conspired."

This **process** of data, warrant, claim, rebuttal, and backing *continues until all argumentation is exhausted.* Then, we add the **qualifier**. The qualifier is *usually an adverb such as "probably," "possibly," "absolutely," etc., which indicates the relative strength of the claim after all arguments are considered.*

In the **second O. J. trial**, the **criminal proceeding**, the prosecution needed to be able to establish a **qualifier** like "*almost definitely*." The **claim** needed to be *proven "beyond a reasonable doubt."* In the **third trial**, the **civil trial**, the **qualifier** needed only to be "*probably*." The *"preponderance of evidence"* (or at least 51 percent probability) was all that the plaintiffs needed to prove. Americans apparently were *divided over the qualifier* in the claim. Virtually everyone could have *agreed that O. J. "possibly" murdered Ron and Nicole.* In fact, what would have been the **first O.J. trial**, the **Grand Jury trial** (which was never held) would have had this type of qualifier. All a prosecutor would have needed to prove to the Grand Jury is that *O. J. "possibly" murdered Ron and Nicole.* Perhaps, O. J.'s defense team was worried that an "indictment" from the grand jury would weaken his chances to win in a criminal trial. The thought may have been that he would rather enter the criminal trial without having lost in any prior trial. Whatever the case, his defense team managed to have the grand jury dismissed, based on the argument that the grand jury had been tainted by the publicity that was given to the case. While most Americans agreed with the qualifier that O.J. "possibly" killed Ron and Nicole, according to polls, most whites thought that he "almost definitely" did. Most blacks disagreed with the "almost definitely" qualifier. They thought there was "reasonable doubt."

Kenneth Burke

Does the *logos* of Toulminian analysis, then, persuade everyone? No. Some are persuaded by the *ethos* of O. J. himself when he claims he didn't do it. Some are so overcome by *pathos*--anger at the murder, pity for Ron and Nicole's family, fear of more racial strife, etc.--that they assume one position or another. Yet, the twentieth century philosopher of human symbol-use Kenneth Burke adds another dimension to the consideration of this issue.

Identification

Burke suggests that there is an element in persuasion that is tied neither to Aristotle's *ethos*, *pathos*, and *logos*, nor to Toulmin's six elements. Burke (1972) calls this element of persuasion **"identification"** (p.27). In my book (1998a), I point out that he subsequently moved his discussion of "identification" into his discussion of **"entelechy."** In the O. J. example, this "identification" element in persuasion revolves around the questions: "To what extent did the black jurors simply want O. J. to win because they identified with him as African-Americans?" and "To what extent did the whites in America simply want O. J. to lose because of his race?" Such a difference in identification can also be seen in political debates that occur each election cycle. Republicans want the Republican candidate to win the debate. Democrats want the Democrat candidate to win the debate. Their conclusions concerning the results of the debates are, therefore, influenced by the **identification** they have with the various candidates. Republicans are more inclined to believe the Republican candidate won. Conversely, Democrats are more inclined to believe the Democrat won. The members of O. J.'s defense team in the criminal trial all actually wore neckties that symbolized black unity. They were attempting to influence the *black* jurors to **identify** with O. J., as a black person. Likewise, the choice of Marcia Clark as lead prosecutor in the criminal trial may well have been designed to influence the predominantly *female* jury that they should **identify** with Nicole, as a woman. Why were black attorneys so prominent on both sides? For that matter, why was the jury predominantly black? What part did the jurors' attitudes toward the Los Angeles Police Department (LAPD) play in the verdict? Did jurors have their own experiences with the LAPD and did these experiences influence their perception of what the LAPD officers did in the Simpson case? How much of this trial was an "us against them" battle? Did the *ethos*, *pathos*, *logos*, data, warrants, claims, rebuttals, backings, and qualifiers even matter? Or, was the outcome of the trial predominantly decided on the basis of **identification**?

Entelechy

At the heart of what Burke sees going on in ("identification" and) **"entelechy"** is a story, a drama, which has both good guys and bad guys. The trick is to tell what story is being experienced in each situation, as interpreted by each person participating. Christians will remember that **Jesus** did virtually all of his persuading by the use of stories (**parables**). The key to understanding each parable is to *discover who you are in the story*. In the story of the Good Samaritan, are you the Jew who was attacked and left to die on the roadway, or are you one of the religious leaders of the Jews who passed by their injured countryman without helping him, or are you the (outsider/stranger) Samaritan who helped the injured Jew? How many people have been persuaded over the years to help a stranger on the roadway, by the sheer force of the Parable of the Good Samaritan? This is **"identification."** So, the questions are: What is the story being experienced? and Who are you in the story? If the **story** that is going on in the mind of a given juror is not "Justice for the Murder of Ron and Nicole" but "Justice for the Beating of Rodney King" (a black man who was video recorded being beaten by the LAPD in the months preceding the O. J. trial), the *criminal who needs to be punished* may be understood to be the LAPD, rather than O. J. If the **story** is a "Brer Rabbit" story, O. J. may be seen as the tricky rabbit who gets caught but always finds a way to escape.

As an **example** of **how entelechy may be used in selling**, on February 10, 2005, an episode of **the Apprentice** aired on NBC-TV. Donald Trump commissioned two teams of would-be apprentices to design and produce a 30-second television commercial for a new product-- a body wash--by the makers of Dove soaps. Donny Deutsch, from the ad agency representing Dove, instructed the teams concerning their task. He explicitly mentioned that the attitude Dove wanted to get across in the commercial was that the new body wash was "refreshing." The two teams floundered and, for the first time since the Apprentice series began, *no team won* the weekly contest. The advertising decision-makers at Dove were thoroughly unimpressed with both attempts.

One team tried to use *sexual innuendo* to sell the product. The team filmed an implicitly pornographic scene of washing a cucumber. This team had no idea of the **brand image** Dove had developed through the years. Their ad, the decision-makers concluded, would be highly offensive to the target market of this product.

The second team used clips of marathon runners sweating and splashing cups of water on themselves, followed by one of the runners smearing the product on his face, splashing it off, and wiping it off with a towel. This runner then won the race. This team, while claiming the misuse of the product was actually a joke, appeared not to even understand **how the product was used**. (The joke bombed.) The thought of smearing the product on the face was considered disgusting. The audience would be turned off, revolted by the ad.

At the end of the episode, Trump showed a clip of the commercial Dove developed independently of the Apprentice. He hailed this as a far superior ad, and it was quite superior to the attempts of the two teams. However, even the Dove ad lacked something. Various (culturally-differentiated) females morphed into other (refreshed?) versions of themselves throughout the ad. The final female who morphed into a different version of herself was Miss Piggy. Although, one might argue that there was some "refreshment" involved in the changes of pictures, the "refreshment" message seem very remote—very vague. Having seen the ad, I am at a loss for why anyone would buy the product. There seemed to be no clear message that "Dove body wash refreshes you." I gathered from one viewing of the ad that the target audience is females--mostly, young (18-30) from various (mostly white, primarily American) cultures. The clip of Miss Piggy at the end is cute, but I don't know what the implicit message is. Is she now representative of those women who will use the product? Are the target market users supposed to **identify** with Miss Piggy? She is a good attention-getter, but the **attention step** is at the very *end of the ad*. Should it not be at the *first of the ad*? Miss Piggy offers no easy implication for the audience as the elderly politician with E.D. Bob Dole does when he shows up at the end of a Pepsi ad featuring a young and attractive Brittany Spears. I am not certain that the audience would easily notice that the commercial is advertising a "body wash," and I do not feel the audience would connect "Dove" with the commercial at all if the commercial were not shown at the end of the Apprentice episode in which the teams were working for Dove. In short, this ad seems to me to be guilty of **vampire creativity** (advertising that *causes one to remember the commercial, but not the product that is being advertised*). As a viewer, I would be more inclined to watch a Muppets movie or visit Disney World after watching the ad than to purchase Dove Cool Moisture Body Wash.

This 30-second ad case cries out for a **story** that could effectively be "**selling entelechy**." **Entelechy** is a term Kenneth Burke adapted from Aristotle. In short, Burke (1970) says: "[W]hereas a beginning, middle, or end must be *explicitly* exactly as it is, each such stage must *implicitly* contain the other two, in anticipation (as regards a beginning), in retrospect (as regards an end), while the middle would somehow contain the 'substance" of both" (p.415). In other words, certain stories are *so well known to us that the mention of just a few words* from the *beginning* of the story such as "Once upon a time" or just a few words from the *end* of the story such as "happily ever after" conjure up quickly in our minds the entire story. If a politician accuses another politician of "crying 'wolf'" regarding an issue, the audience conjures up the entire story of the boy who cried wolf.

Brief ads such as the Dove ad would benefit greatly from entelechial selling. Think of the stories everyone knows that involve a "refreshing" of sorts. The clearest example that comes to my mind is "**Snow White** [SW]." Imagine an ad that begins with the scene of Snow White **lying in repose in a glass coffin in a forest**. Everyone watching implicitly *knows the entire story from* *just this one piece of information.* The audience expects the handsome prince to come and awaken her with the kiss of love. However, since it is a forest scene, the camera focuses on a **Dove** flittering out of the sky. The dove lands on SW's coffin, opens the lid, and **becomes a bottle of Dove Cool Moisture Body Wash** in the hand of SW. She very sleepily drags herself out of the coffin and heads to a nearby **waterfall** where she is **refreshed**. Now wide awake, refreshed, clean, and dressed, she looks up to see the prince coming toward her. She happily cries, "Prince!" and the commercial ends.

Does the audience get the picture that it was the Dove Cool Moisture Body Wash that "refreshed" her? Yes. Do they remember the **brand name—Dove**? You bet. Is the story offensive to the target audience? I don't think so. Many in the audience may love the story of Snow White and will **identify** with SW as she is ready to take on anything after her morning body wash. Even if the audience contains feminists who might be *offended* by the fairy tale genre, this *story reduces the role of the male prince*. It is the **"Dove"** that **refreshed SW**.

Another example of entelechy is the Walt Disney movie *Pinocchio*. Audiences are able to pick up on what is good vs. what is bad without even being told to do one thing and not to do another:

- For Pinocchio, going to school is good; truancy is bad.
- Telling the truth is good; lying causes one's nose to grow.
- Gambling, Drinking alcohol, smoking, and playing pool are in the bad cluster of self-indulgence (engaged in a scene called "Pleasure Island"); unselfishly risking oneself in attempt to save Gepetto from the whale is good.

The eventual result of bad behavior is gradual transformation into a donkey and being sold to work in the salt mines; the result of good behavior is transformation into a real boy. It is unnecessary to explicitly preach the sermons:

- Thou shalt not be truant.
- Thou shalt not lie.

- Thou shalt not gamble.

- Thou shalt not drink alcohol.

- Thou shalt not smoke.

- Thou shalt not play pool.

The entelechy accomplishes the preaching for us. Since we don't want to become donkeys and we do want to be real, **we subconsciously persuade ourselves** to follow the **implicit** sermons. **Explicitly**, Pinocchio had been told early on, by the Blue Fairy, that he would become a real boy, if he proved himself "brave, truthful, and unselfish." Disney's *Pinocchio* thus **explicitly** exhibits the **values** Disney wishes to present. It is unnecessary for Disney to point out those times Pinocchio was brave, truthful, and unselfish. The audience sees the values exhibited in the story. As Burke suggests, humans *subconsciously act upon themselves* in accordance with the implicit value systems of the entelechies/stories with which they identify. Hence, **values are transmitted**. As in the Pinocchio entelechy, humans generally identify positively with **unselfish** and **truthful** persons. As in the Parable of the Good Samaritan, humans generally identify positively with **individuals who help others**. Humans do **not** identify with **individuals who take advantage of others**.

I recommend that salespersons try to **control the identification of the story** that is being lived out in the sales interview. This is done by placing the sale within the context of an appropriate entelechy. Certainly, the entelechy/story of "*The Villainous Salesperson Who Is Lying in an Attempt to Take the Poor Prospect's Money*" is **not** the story that we want to present. Our entelechy should not be one in which with **salespersons take advantage of others**. Instead, we need to supply a different entelechy for the prospect—in which **we are seen as helping others**--or the *Villainous Salesperson* entelechy may persist. I discuss this issue specifically in **Sale Number Six**, **Twelve**, and **Twenty-One**.

Organizing the Twenty-One Sales

Having considered some of the contributions to the art of persuasion offered by Socrates, Plato, Aristotle, Jesus, Richard Weaver, Stephen Toulmin, and Kenneth Burke, I turn to the premise upon which this book is based. There are **twenty-one sales** (or persuasion issues) **within a typical sale**. The remainder of this book will delineate these twenty-one sales and offer suggestions for approaching each sale. Since each of these persuasion issues may be considered a separate sale, each sale should be organized separately. In the remainder of this chapter, I present my system for organizing each sale.

I call my system "**The Focus System**." By using this title, I intend to suggest that most people who make attempts at persuasion are "unfocused." Salespersons need to **focus on one sales objective at a time**. Imagine the outline of a ping pong paddle. If this outline were fuzzy and out of focus, what else might that outline resemble? A light bulb? A bicycle seat? An alien's head (ET phone home)? The thought bubble from a cartoon? A funnel? A tennis racket? A golf tee? A balloon?

What if I told you that it was **not a ping pong paddle** standing upright on its handle? What if I brought the picture more nearly into focus and you could see two large lines extending up from the narrow (handle) end to divide the wide end roughly into thirds? What if you then saw smaller lines branching off of the two large lines, then lines that are smaller still branching off of the smaller lines? You begin to see a **tree**. If I were to write on the subject of trees, you *might* say that my paper was focused. No longer am I writing about ping pong paddles, thought bubbles, aliens, and bicycle seats; I am writing about one subject--trees--but am I really focused? Consider the following paragraph on trees:

> *I think that I shall never see a poem lovely as a tree. Trees are great! When I was a kid, I had a big old tree in my back yard. We tied a rope to one of the limbs and a tire to the other end of the rope. I loved to swing on that tire swing. Today, I ate corn on the cob and had a kernel lodged between my teeth. I used a piece of a tree, a toothpick, to*

dislodge the corn. Birds live in trees. You know that if they cut down all of the rain forests, there will be no more oxygen on the earth. When I was young, my girlfriend and I carved our initials in the bark of a tree. She later injured her leg and had to use crutches--made from trees. Leaves come in several colors--green, red, yellow, blue, brown. I hate getting hit with baseball bats. Has that ever happened to you? In the summer, I like to sit in the shade, under a tree. In conclusion, trees have roots.

Clearly, this paragraph **stays on the subject** of trees, but it is **not focused**. Many sales presentations are similarly unfocused. The salesperson offers numerous pieces of data, claims, warrants, backing, etc. concerning his/her product. Since all pieces of data, etc. pertain to the product, the salesperson feels that s/he has stayed on the subject. Indeed, some of the pieces of data may even have persuasive power, but the prospect is forced to search for those nuggets of persuasion as a prospector might pan for gold. **By clearly organizing your data**, you do much to make certain that your prospect understands the **evidence that a problem exists**, the **main cause(s) of the problem**, the available **solutions**, the **efficacy of those solutions**, and the **feasibility of those solutions**. Hence, you eliminate much of the **competence stress** that the prospect may otherwise feel. You avoid **confusion stress**. You make it much easier for your prospect to make a purchasing decision.

I have used the focus system an organizing principle **for this book as a whole and to organize each sale that must be made**. I believe that by mastering the focus system, you will make your sales presentations clearer and, thus, make more sales. There are **eight elements in a focus**. They are:

- **subject**: the broad topic;
- **theme**: some aspect of the subject;
- **proposition**: the most important statement you wish to make about the theme;
- **interrogative**: the one-word question which the audience will ask upon hearing the proposition;

- **key word**: the one noun which best categorizes the list you will provide to the audience after they ask the interrogative;

- **audience**: the person(s) you are addressing;

- **objective**: your purpose in addressing this audience;

- **divisions**: the specific list, categorized by your key word, which will organize your presentation.

If you fully consider all eight of these elements of focus for each of the twenty-one sales, your presentation should be well-organized and focused.

Some tips will help to make the use of the focus system easy. I will demonstrate the system by using the subject, "trees." This subject is chosen for **illustrative purposes only**. My goal at this point is only to demonstrate how focus works as an organizational principle. However, if you are employed by a tree nursery or lumber yard, some parts of this example may actually be useful in that your sales.

To *narrow the subject to a theme*, we use the **three elements of a theme**: a *plural noun*, the *word "of" or the word "for,"* and the *subject*. Since the **subject** in our example is "*trees*," we look for a *plural noun* to place *before the words "of trees" or "for trees"* that will narrow our subject. Examples of themes might be: colors of trees, species of trees, uses of trees, sizes of trees, products of trees, purposes for trees, etc.

The **plural noun** that we choose to begin our theme becomes our **key word**. A *key word is always a plural noun*. Since it *categorizes a list* which we will supply as our **divisions**, it must be plural. Consider the category "colors." The list of divisions might include green, blue, red, yellow, orange, etc. Under the category "species," we may list oak, walnut, fir, redwood, maple, etc.

Not every plural noun will sufficiently narrow our subject for a brief presentation. We could try the category "leaves" (thus, making the theme: "leaves of trees"), but this would probably not be narrow enough. There are trillions and trillions of leaves on earth. We could not begin to consider each one in a presentation. On the other hand *by making our key word "uses"* (and our **theme**: "uses of trees"), we are somewhat more focused. We could *list the "uses"*--fuel, oxygen, shade, landscape, houses, boats, baseball bats, toothpicks, fruit bearing, wind breaks, tables, floors, beds, decks, fences, habitat for animals, playground equipment, etc. Unfortunately, this is *still not narrow enough*. The "theme" is too large unless we wish to write a book on the uses of trees.

Let's **try changing the subject** from "trees" to "lumber." Now, with *"uses" as our key word* and *"lumber" as our subject*, we have the following *theme: "uses of lumber."* There are basically three uses of lumber: interior, exterior, and framing. For framing houses, people use cheap, straight, soft lumber like pine. For interior uses such as hardwood floors, furniture, cabinets, and trim, people use hardwoods like oak, walnut, and cherry. For exterior uses, like decks, fences, picnic tables, gym sets, shingles, and siding, people use good weathering lumbers like redwood and cedar.

The **proposition**, as previously mentioned, is the *primary statement one wishes to make about the theme*. With "uses of lumber" as our theme, I can make *the following proposition*: "There are three basic uses of lumber."

The **interrogative** is a *one-word question* that the audience would likely ask upon hearing the proposition. There are **six interrogatives**: *who, what, when, where, why,* and *how*. However, I must choose just one of those six. If my audience hears the proposition, "There are three basic uses of lumber," they will probably ask, "What?" Do not elaborate; it should be evident what the audience is asking by **just using the "one word."** Of course, here, they mean What (are the three uses), but *do not add* the words "are the three uses."

The **key word** is the plural noun that categorizes each item in the list of divisions. If I say, "There are three basic uses of lumber," and my audience asks, "What?" I will answer them by listing the three "uses." "Uses" is, thus, my key word. **In oral communication, it is important to use the key word every time a division is introduced.** This helps the audience keep track of the basic structure of the presentation. Each **transition between divisions** should contain a

number and the **key word**. For example, "The **first use** of lumber is for framing." The presenter can even provide an **internal summary** in the process of making a transition, such as: "Now that we have considered the first two uses, framing and interior, let's consider the third and final use, exterior."

The **divisions** are the *specific elements of the list that is thus generated*. In the list of "uses," *my three divisions* are: (1) framing, (2) interior, and (3) exterior. These divisions organize the presentation on the uses of lumber.

The **audience** is the specific person or group to whom the presentation is directed. In my example, an appropriate audience might be *do-it-yourselfers*.

The **objective** always **starts with the word "to"** *followed* usually by *either* the word "*inform*" or the word "*persuade*." In most of your sales, the word "persuade" will be used. In our example, we use the word "inform." The *third word* of your objective will be your *audience* (e.g., "do-it-yourselfers"). The *fourth word* is "*that*." The *rest of your objective* is your "*proposition*." A **full objective looks like this**: "To inform do-it-yourselfers that there are three basic uses of lumber."

In preparation for this book, I used the following focus:

Subject: A typical sale.

Theme: Sales of a typical sale.

Proposition: There are twenty-one sales in a typical sale.

Interrogative: What?

Key Word: Sales.

Audience: Salespersons and Sales Managers.

Objective: To inform Salespersons and Sales Managers that there are twenty-one sales in a typical sale.

Divisions:

    1. Self: There is a need for my product: a problem exists

2. Self: My product is a proper solution for the need/problem

3. Self: I am the right person to sell this solution

4. Self: I should do market research

5. Self: I should call my prospects

6. Phone Prospect: You should give me just one minute of your time

7. Phone Prospect: This matter is relevant to you

8. Phone Prospect: I am a legitimate enterprise

9. Phone Prospect: It is worthwhile for you to consider more information on this subject

10. Prospect: You have a problem/need

11. Prospect: I am well-qualified to help you

12. Prospect: I have a proposal worth considering

13. Prospect: You should agree to become a decision-maker

14. Decision-maker: My proposal addresses the cause of your problem

15. Decision-maker: My proposal will solve your problem

16. Decision-maker: My proposal is feasible

17. Decision-maker: My proposal will help to solve other problems

18. Decision-maker: You should enact my proposal

19. Client: You should accept delivery of my solution

20. Client: You should continue to be my client

21. Client: You should provide a reference for me

Integrated Marketing Communication (IMC)

These twenty-one divisions serve as the chapters of this book. My major goal as author of *Making offers they can't refuse* is to present **Marketing Communication** centering on a thorough **business proposal approach** as an honorable, ethical, and successful profession. If you are totally **thorough** in the presentation of your case, you will be using the art of rhetoric

ethically. By identifying every necessary persuasive step in a direct Personal Selling situation, *I am encouraging you to be thorough.* **Personal Selling**, or **Personal Sales**, is the most thorough form of marketing communication. I use Personal Sales as the skeleton upon which to introduce other forms of **Integrated Marketing Communication [IMC]** in this book.

Throughout the text, various comments will apply the principles learned in most chapters to the field of IMC. **IMC** is an approach that *recognizes that all types of Marketing Communication used by a business or organization should be coordinated, in order to produce the most effective marketing results.* Clearly, the more coordinated the Marketing Communication messages delivered by a business or organization, the more effective the overall marketing message will be. Among the **types of Marketing Communication** included in IMC are:

- **Advertising** (traditionally, the primary mass media form),
- **Public Relations** (often, the attempt to receive mass media coverage without fees),
- **Personal Sales** (the central skeletal approach of this book),
- **Promotions** (providing opportunities, incentives, and stimuli for "trying" the product now),
- **Packaging** (the messages sent by the way the product is packaged),
- **Sponsorships** (reputation enhancement provided by sponsoring events, etc.), and
- **Direct Marketing** (through catalogs, infomercials, telemarketing, internet, etc.).
- **Online Marketing** (through the internet).
- **Mobile Marketing** (through cellphones and similar devices).
- **Diffusion of Innovations** (through word of mouth).

Of these, **Advertising** has often been describes as **above-the-line**, suggesting that it is the primary form of marketing communication, while **all others** are described as **below-the-line**. **With the advent of IMC, all types** of Marketing Communication are *considered on more of an equal level. This is called **through-the-line** Marketing Communication.*

High vs. Low Involvement

The **primary difference** between **Personal Sales** and the other types of Marketing Communication is that *Personal Sales often must take into account <u>every single step</u> in Marketing Communication.* **Other types** of Marketing Communication *may apply variously to some of the steps, but not to others.* Hence, **Personal Selling is used** in what **Consumer Behavior** experts call "**high involvement**" decisions. High involvement decisions are *those that are **not** typically made on the spur of the moment.* Decisions *that **are** typically made on the spur of the moment* are termed "**low involvement**" decisions—the purchase of a candy bar, salty snack, hand soap for the bathroom, those extra treats and paraphernalia one finds beside in the check-out line at Walmart. Such **impulsive sales** *do **not** require the services of a full-fledged salesperson.* However, **most insurance products**—*life* insurance, *health* insurance, *disability* insurance, *car* insurance, *homeowners* insurance, *contractor's liability* insurance, *crop* insurance, *earthquake* insurance, *errors and omissions* insurance, *flood* insurance, *malpractice* insurance *marine* insurance, *renter's* insurance, *title* insurance, *etc.—require high involvement decisions.*

High involvement decisions **typically** (1) involve the **outlay of substantial sums of money** and (2) **require the consideration of many factors**. The (3) **specifics of the purchase** are also, typically, **more difficult to understand**. What, if anything, is required by the government or the lender/mortgage company? What deductible should I choose? What specific coverages do I need? How much does each element cost? What are my options for making payments? Therefore, **other** purchases that are usually **high involvement purchases** are **automobiles, boats, recreational vehicles, farm implements, business machines, computers**, other **high-tech equipment** and **software programs, retirement plans, investments, college degree programs, private elementary and high schools, diet plans, vacation plans, condominium time-shares, real estate, construction services, landscaping services, house painting services, remodeling**, etc.

Not every purchase that involves the *outlay of substantial sums of money* is, however, a *high involvement* purchase. As gas prices hovered around $4.00/gallon, the purchase of gas for your car became a high-ticket purchase on a regular basis, yet, most people do not consult a full-fledged salesperson to make decisions about gas purchases. We just pull into the pumps of some convenient (and fairly competitive) station. Even though **substantial cash outlays are involved**, this is a **low involvement** purchase. Not every sale that does **not** involve the outlay of substantial sums of money is a low involvement purchase. If a "persuader" attempts to persuade you to become a member of his *church, mosque, synagogue,* or *political party*, and thoroughly discusses all of the reasons and ramifications for your decision, you are in a **high involvement** sale, even if **no cash outlay** is involved.

As you consider a sales career, be sure to consider whether the career involves high involvement or low involvement decisions. Personal Selling is generally needed **only in high involvement situations**. Personal Selling, with your **income dependent on commissions**, is not only **capable of providing a much greater income** than salaried positions provide, it is the **closest you come to being an entrepreneur** without opening a business yourself. Especially in **economic downturns**, *Personal Selling* skill **offers opportunities** that can keep you from the throes of unemployment. Even *if you are reading this text primarily as a guide to work your way through all of the persuasion that occurs in the marketing process*, it will, by extension, **make you more secure economically** by teaching you **survival skills** in case of *economic downturns.*

Using Personal Sales as a guide for working through the entire marketing/persuasion process yields a much more thorough approach to Marketing Communication than can be afforded by any other type of Marketing Communication. As we work through the steps of Personal Sales, we will relate the other "through-the-line" types of Marketing Communication to the sales principles. We will now consider each of the twenty-one sales--one by one. We will consider the focus (or organization) of each sale as well as the available means of making each sale.

In **Part One**, you begin with the most honest and ethical of sales steps, the five sales to yourself (the ***intra*personal sales**). When you begin the sales process by selling yourself, there is a spirit of total candor at work. It is difficult to conceal truth from yourself. You must be willing to take into account serious counter arguments (or *rebuttals*). You will learn to use the logical method of **Stephen Toulmin**. You must search to discover *data*. You must think to determine the specific *warrants* that drive you to make *claims* based upon the data. You must provide *backing*, when a rebuttal surfaces. This is thoroughness. When you have exhausted the possible arguments, you must become a fair judge. You must apply the correct *qualifier* to the claim.

In **Part Two**, you move to the first ***inter*personal** contact. The entire group of four sales typically takes only one minute to accomplish. Therefore, virtually every word that is uttered (or visual symbol used) must contain a great deal of **implicit persuasion**. The **primary implicit message** that is being conveyed is *that you are courteous and competent*. This telephone contact helps to establish *initial ethos*. Responsibly and courteously, you ask for *only one minute* of time. Once the minute is granted, you quickly establish the *relevance* of the subject to the phone prospect and *present the legitimacy of the business entity* for dealing with the subject. You hope that *this one minute* conversation will persuade the phone prospect that *it is worthwhile for him/her to consider more information on the subject*. This one-minute Personal Selling example is the **paradigm for one-minute television or radio ads**, or even **print ads**, **outdoor ads**, **internet ads**, etc. Sometimes, a great deal can be accomplished in *only one minute*, or even less! But, **one-minute ads or phone calls alone cannot complete the process**.

In **Part Three**, the *phone prospect* has become a **legitimate prospect**. S/he has expressed some level of *interest in receiving information on the topic*. The **first three of the four sales** that are made to the prospect at this stage **may be accomplished by technological means**. I personally have used *print*, *audio*, and *audio-visual* presentation technologies to accomplish these three sales. I do **not advise** sales persons to use recordings to accomplish the sales to the phone prospect, although, computerized phone contacts are being tried, with some success, by various business entities. I think the **first contact should be personal**. But, now that some interest has been expressed, it is often *expedient* and more *convenient for all involved* to accomplish the next three sales technologically. You need to persuade the prospect **that s/he has a problem**. The prospect must be persuaded **that you and your business entity are well qualified to help** the prospect and th**at you have a** *proposal* **for helping the prospect that is worth considering.**

The final sale of **Part Three** must be made **in person**. Much has been said about the importance of *treating the prospect ethically*. Here, not only do you treat the prospect ethically, but also the ***prospect learns to treat you ethically***. It is **unethical** for a prospect to **consume your time and teaching if** the prospect knows all along that s/he will not make a decision. S/he *need not promise to make a positive decision*. It is up to you to persuade the prospect that a positive decision is the proper one. Yet, it is only courteous for the prospect to **let you know whether or not a decision will be made upon becoming fully informed. You are ethical** because *you provide forewarning that a decision will be expected* upon the completion of the thorough presentation of the proposal. There is *no concealing of the truth*, here. You are being completely *honest and above-board*. If the prospect is unwilling to become a decision-maker, today, **you and the prospect negotiate the time frame for the decision to be made**. Since the prospect will forget many details over time, the detailed presentation is delayed until the prospect is willing to become a decision-maker.

In **Part Four**, the prospect has become a **decision-maker**. This is a very professional context. The five sales in this part comprise nothing less than a **legitimate business proposal**. The scene might just as well be the board room of a Fortune 500 company. You must keep this **entelechy** in mind. (As mentioned, at the heart of what **Kenneth Burke** sees going on in "entelechy" is a story. The trick is to tell what story is being lived in each situation, as interpreted by each person participating. The key to understanding entelechy is to discover who you are in the story.)   In this case, remember that **the story** is *not a sale*, it **is a business proposal**. You are presenting a *proposal*, not a product.   You are inducing the decision-maker to become your *client*, not customer.   You employ *causal analysis* to demonstrate that your proposal is not a "Band-Aid" approach.   You provide statistics, case studies, and anecdotal evidence that *your proposal works*. You address the four *feasibility* issues.   You suggest other incidental problems that the proposal may also help to solve.   This is a thorough proposal.   Upon completion, you--the professional-- recommend to the decision-maker: "You should enact my proposal." **Now, the decision-maker has a *choice*. S/he may say yes or no.** The word *maybe* was eliminated earlier. Whatever the decision, you must **accept it graciously**.   The agreement was that a decision would be made. The agreement has been honored. All involved have been ethical. Many decisions will be positive. Hence, frequently, the decision-maker will become your **client**.

In **Part Five**, three final sales remain to be made. 1) The *solution* (i.e., product) must be *delivered*. 2) The long-term professional-client relationship must be solidified. 3) And, the professional courtesy of providing a *reference* must be requested. This is a time to **fully establish the *business entelechy*** that has been developed throughout *Making offers they can't refuse*. It is no time to bring the entelechy crashing down. It is no time to change the entelechy from the business entelechy to the sales entelechy. Your future depends upon your reputation. It is a valuable commodity. As a professional, you want your client to supply the positive reputation that comes from having completed a thoroughly professional process.

In closing this chapter on sales theory, I point once more to the **first sentence of this chapter**: *Sales is nothing more than persuasion with the implication that the exchange of money is involved*. This means that the historic principles of persuasion may be systematically applied to all areas of sales. It also means, however, that this book on sales may be applied as a systematic method of accomplishing virtually any type of persuasion. The sales example offered may be viewed as simply an illustration of how persuasion works. Even if the exchange of money is not involved, *Making offers they can't refuse* will be useful to anyone who would **persuade successfully and ethically**.

TWENTY-ONE SALES: PART ONE

AUDIENCE = SELF

SALE NUMBER ONE

There is a Need for My Product: A Problem Exists

Subject: The problem.

Theme: Proofs of the problem.

Proposition: There are proofs that a problem exists.

Interrogative: What?

Key Word: Proofs.

Audience: Self.

Objective: To persuade myself that there are proofs that a problem exists (i.e., there is a need for my product).

Divisions (i.e., "proofs"):

    1. Facts

    2. Statistics

    3. Authorities

    4. Anecdotes

    5. Case Studies

    6. Scenarios

The year was 1979. I was in the process of completing the last of my coursework for the Ph.D. at the University of Illinois when one of my professors invited me to his apartment for a coke. I suppose that I was anticipating a plush setting. I had assumed that holding the Ph.D. degree and a tenure-track faculty appointment at a Big Ten university translated into a sizable income. I was wrong. The apartment was inexpensive and modestly furnished. My professor informed me that he was earning only $12,000 per year. (Adjusted for inflation, this amount would equal approximately $40,000 per year in 2015.)

I could not believe it. Why had I spent so many years in graduate school? Why had I invested so much in tuition and fees? I certainly could not afford to raise my four children on that amount of income. Was the salary scale at the University of Illinois below that of other universities?

No.

I came to the conclusion that a career as a college professor would not pay a comfortable wage. But what other careers were available to me? I searched the want ads but found nothing attractive . . . except a sales position.

The company that placed the advertisement was seeking a well-educated individual to market financial products to college seniors and graduate students. I called for an interview. I was offered a position in which my first year's income was projected to be $30,000. (Adjusted for inflation, this amount would equal approximately $98,000 per year in 2015.) This sounded better to me than the $12,000/year salary of a college teacher and, since I had received an offer to teach college courses on a part-time basis in the city in which I would be working, I considered the offer a godsend. I could teach college, as I desired, and still earn a comfortable wage.

The **first sale of my career** was at my doorstep. Could I persuade myself to forego plans to teach college full-time and turn, instead, to a sales career? **Three questions** came immediately to mind: *(1) Is there a need for the product that the company wants me to market? (2) Is the company's product a proper solution for the need?* and *(3) Am I the right person to sell this solution?* Answering these three questions for myself constituted the **first three sales** of what I would later term: "The Twenty-One Sales in a Sale."

These three sales (as well as the two sales that follow them) are what I call "**intrapersonal sales**." *Inter*personal **communication** exists when there is communication between two humans. *Intrapersonal* **communication** is that *communication which one has with oneself*. There is *little chance of deceiving my audience*, since *I* am my audience.

In some respects, selling something to myself is **more difficult than selling to others**. I certainly *cannot hide the weak points in my argument* from myself. I *cannot use purely emotional appeals* that overlook logical considerations--my audience will see right through such tactics. I *cannot lie to myself* regarding facts, statistics, case studies, anecdotes, and authoritative claims. **In short, I am forced to be ethical** in my dealings with myself. Hence, this is great place to begin practicing ethical persuasion! I can learn a lot about the way in which I may ethically persuade others by observing myself in these "intrapersonal sales."

In other respects, selling something to myself is **easier than making a sale to someone else**. *I have **ethos** for myself*. I trust myself to be honest, to have active goodwill towards myself, and I know the exact amount of expertise that I possess. Later, I will need to persuade my interpersonal audiences that I have these characteristics, but in these "intrapersonal sales," the *ethos* is already established.

Not only do I qualify in these sales as an ethical persuader, I may *also* qualify as a *well-informed judge* (or audience). True, there are times when we say that we "deceive ourselves," but usually what we mean is that we are so influenced by one factor that we tend to diminish the importance of contrary factors. As a judge, I may be influenced by my desires, but I am usually still well-informed. To make certain that I, as a judge, am well-informed, *I apply the Toulminian method to my intrapersonal sales*. I will provide examples of Toulminian analysis as I use my own situation for illustrative purposes.

English composition specialists Axelrod and Cooper (1994) offer **six basic types of evidence** for constructing arguments--*facts, statistics, authorities, anecdotes, scenarios,* and *cases* (p.538). It is useful to consider each of these kinds of evidence in order.

Facts

Facts are *statements with which no reasonable person would disagree*. They are useful as *premises for syllogisms* or as *warrants* and *data* in the Toulminian system. I recommend that the salesperson list all pertinent facts that might relate to the perceived problem that is under consideration. Since the position that was being offered to me in 1979 was primarily life insurance sales, I could list the following pertinent facts:

1. Everybody dies sooner or later. (No one disagrees with this, so it makes a good fact.)

2. There are expenses when people die (funeral services, casket, grave site, final medical expenses, monument, etc.).

3. Family and friends do not typically try to get by cheaply on these expenses when death occurs.

4. Not every person who dies has available cash to pay for these expenses.

5. Many who die have others who depend on them.

Once I have listed some facts to be used as **data**, I might consider some facts that could be used as **warrants**. While the term *data* refers to *specific facts*, the term *warrant* refers to *generalized truths*. Toulmin (1964) suggests that the word **"since"** is **quite useful when composing warrants** (p. 99). I should *try stating the data, followed by the word "since" and a general statement of truth (warrant)*. This might, in turn, produce a **claim**. An example might be: "*You will die sooner or later* (**data**). *Since people should be prepared for events which they know will happen* (**warrant**), *you should be prepared for death* (**claim**)."

My **warrant is a fact**. It is a statement with which no reasonable person would disagree. *People should be prepared for events which they know will happen.* If I know that I will have to teach a class or give a speech tomorrow, I should be prepared. If I know that the temperature in Alaska will be sub-zero when my plane arrives, I should bring some heavy clothing. If I know that the grass in my lawn will grow every summer, I should buy a mower or contract to have the mowing done. I cannot think of a single event that I know will happen to me for which I should not be prepared.

Secondly, my **warrant is a general statement.** It applies not only to the specific case of dying, but also to many other specific cases--teaching a class, giving a speech, arriving in Alaska, mowing my lawn, etc. Hence, it is a general statement: *People should be prepared for events which they know will happen.*

Thirdly, my **warrant suggests a claim.** Since people should be prepared for events that they know will happen, *people should be prepared for death.* Does this claim help me sell myself on the proposition that "there are proofs that a problem exists (i.e., there is a need for my product)"? Of course, it does. What about the other facts that I had listed above? Can they be linked with warrants in order to produce useful claims?

Let's try the second **fact (or piece of data):** *There are expenses when people die (funeral services, casket, grave site, final medical expenses, monument, etc.). Since expenses require money to pay them* (warrant), *people need money when they die* (claim). Again, my piece of **data** is a fact and it is general. What expenses are handled without money? Does the **claim**, *People need money when they die*, help me sell myself on the proposition that "there are proofs that a problem exists"?

The third **fact** is: *Family and friends do not typically try to get by cheaply on these expenses when death occurs.* When my audience changes from myself to prospects, some will disagree with this piece of data. It is an attempt at **sales resistance**. However, since I am my own audience, here, I can admit the truth to myself. If a family member says at my death, "Throw him in a box and cover him with dirt and forget him," s/he is being rather insensitive. Family members may resist extravagance, but they typically spend enough money to send the message that we love this person and are sending him away with dignity. I may move to my **warrant**: *Since it is not good for me to ask my family and friends to pay my bills.* Anyone could add the claim: *I should have enough money available at my death to pay for at least moderate expenses.*

The fourth **fact/data** is that *not every person who dies has available cash to pay for these expenses.* Some do, I must admit to myself. But just the fact that some do does not negate the fact that *not every person* who dies does. My warrant: *Since people should have enough money available at their death to pay for at least 'moderate' expenses* . . . (and my claim) *those who do not have available cash to pay for these expenses need money at the time of their death.* Note that my **warrant**, this time, comes essentially from my **claim** in the previous paragraph. I can do this because all claims that have been established through syllogistic reasoning (and that is what Toulminian analysis uses in data, warrant, and claim) may be considered to be facts. Note also that I have just accomplished, using only facts and Toulmin's first three elements the objective of **Sale Number One**: To persuade myself that there are proofs that a problem exists (i.e., there is a need for my product).

Before we move on, let's consider that **final fact**: *Many who die have others who depend on them.* *Since the term **depend**, according to* Webster's Seventh New Collegiate Dictionary (*hereafter*, Webster's) *means "to place reliance or trust . . . esp[ecially] for financial support"* (**warrant**), *many who die leave others who need financial support* (claim). These others who had placed *reliance or trust . . . for financial support* in someone who has just died have a problem. I restate my **proposition**: There are proofs that a problem exists.

Statistics

According to *Webster's*, **statistics** is that *"branch of mathematics dealing with the collection, analysis, interpretation, and presentation of masses of numerical data."* In the discussion of *logos* in the Introduction, I link *statistics* with *inductive reasoning.* Statistics are nothing more than *the accumulation of a number of examples from which we draw conclusions.* Since my primary market as a life insurance agent was to be college seniors and graduate students, some *statistics* that were significant in accomplishing the objective of **Sale Number One**, according to my personal example, were:

1. Ninety-five percent of the college seniors and graduate students (at a specific university) are between the ages of 21 and 30.

2. Eighty percent of the college seniors and graduate students (at a specific university) are not married.

3. The statistical probability that someone between the ages of 21 and 30 will die in a given year is slightly less than 2 per 1000, according to the 1956 CSO mortality tables.

4. Among young men between ages 15 and 24, suicide and motor vehicle accidents account for one-half of all deaths, among young women in the same age group, they account for over 40 percent.[2]

5. Seventy-five percent of the college seniors and graduate students (at a specific university) are unemployed or minimally employed.

Rather than repeating the data-warrant-claim procedure that I followed in my discussion of facts, I might attempt to use the **rebuttal-backing** procedure here. Recall that *any data, warrant, claim, or backing may be rebutted*, and that a rebuttal typically *begins with the word "unless."* Furthermore, *I may provide backing to counter any rebuttal.* The backing typically *begins with the word "but."* Let's try it.

Rebutting the fact that *everybody dies sooner or later*, I have had clients add, **unless** *Jesus returns in my lifetime* (**rebuttal**). Fair enough. I like to have Christian clients. I would respond, ***But***, *statistically, you cannot count on that event happening* (**backing**). *Christians have been anticipating the return of Christ for nearly the past 2000 years* (**statistics**). *There is no guarantee that He will return in your lifetime, let alone this year.*

Since my target market would consist of students, I might anticipate some of them **rebutting my earlier warrant**--*since it is not good for me to ask my family and friends to pay my bills.* Students might say, **unless** *I am still a dependent of my parents and they are accustomed to*

---

[2]Victor Fuchs, "Suicide Among Young People," reprinted in Axelrod and Cooper (1994), p. 352.

paying my bills (**rebuttal**). My **backing** might be, ***But**, you are 21* (or more) *years of age* (**statistic** #1 above), *and it is time for you to exercise some independence.*

Many of my prospects may try to **rebut the fifth piece of data** which I offered: *Many who die have others who depend on them.* They may say, ***unless** I am still unmarried* (**rebuttal**), as 80 percent of them are (**statistic** #2). My **backing** might be: ***but**, statistically, you will be married within the next few years.* An **alternative backing** might be: ***but**, your parents depend on you more than you realize.*

They may **rebut the fact** that *everybody dies sooner or later*, by saying ***unless**, statistically, it is much more likely that I will die later, rather than sooner.* I would acknowledge this point. In all honesty, the statistical probability that one of these clients will die this year is only 2 out of 1,000. Yet, I would still add the **backing**: ***but**, statistically, there are 6,000 graduating students, this year, at this university. This means that as many as 12 of you could die, this year. What if you happen to be one of the 12?*

They may **rebut the backing** that I just presented by saying, ***unless** most of those 12 who may die have serious illnesses now, and I am not ill* (**rebuttal**). To which I may reply, ***but**, statistically, suicide and motor vehicle accidents account for one-half of all deaths among young men between ages 15 and 24. Among young women, they account for over 40 percent of deaths. If you assume that the number of deaths which might be pertinent to you is only four or five, and you drive or ride in a motor vehicle, your death is still a serious possibility* (**backing**).

Finally, some in my target market might **rebut the warrant**: ***since** people should have enough money available at their death to pay for at least moderate expenses.* A student might offer, ***unless** I am unemployed or minimally employed right now* (as 75 percent of the students in my market are), *and I do not even have money to pay for living expenses, let alone dying expenses* (**rebuttal**). In my situation, I had a **backing** for this quite convincing **rebuttal**. My company offered a promissory note that would pay for the insurance until the student had graduated and was earning an income. At that time, the student would begin paying (and repaying the note). Therefore, I could offer this **backing**: *but, you will be employed very soon, and until then, you do not need to make payments.*

Authorities

Authorities are *those who have sufficient **ethos** for the audience to be able to advise the audience.* Recall that *ethos* requires both expertise and active good will. Who would know whether or not a problem exists which my product might help solve? Who would have enough active goodwill toward me to honestly level with me? Representatives of the insurance company that was recruiting me certainly had the expertise, but they faced the same **rebuttal** that I would later face when talking to prospects: *unless you have a conflict of interest which causes you to be less than honest with me.* I will deal with the matter of providing backing for this rebuttal later. For now, I am still searching for **someone who might possess total** *ethos*.

Here, for example, I might turn to the United States government. I realize that this authority does not possess *ethos* for every audience, but **I** am the audience, in this instance. Clearly, the U.S. Government believes that a problem exists. One of the provisions of the Social Security program is a death benefit, however small. It could be counter-argued, *unless this is just an excuse by the government to collect additional taxes* (**rebuttal**). *But, the tax codes provide many tax benefits for those who own private life insurance* (**backing**). There would be no advantage to the government in providing tax breaks to individuals who own private life insurance. And the government, most definitely, knows the extent of the problem. Hence, the government has *ethos*. It has **expertise** on the matter as well as **active goodwill** towards the citizenry. The government apparently wants citizens to have protection in this area, even if that means it will collect fewer taxes!

Anecdotes

An **anecdote** is *a true story drawn from the speaker's actual life experience* or, at least, an experience of which the speaker has first-hand knowledge. Since the speaker has first-hand knowledge of the information presented, clearly the speaker possesses *expertise* regarding the story. **The speaker possesses *ethos*.** Since the story is true, it serves as an example of the type of situation under consideration. Therefore, **the story is** an application of *inductive reasoning*, which is **a type of *logos*.** Most importantly, since an anecdote puts the principle that is being explained into a real life situation with real people who may have experienced the problem that exists, **an anecdote provides *pathos*.** It supplies **emotion**, a powerful means of persuasion.[3]

Unfortunately, most of us have heard stories about young people who have lost their lives all too often. But, this sale is a sale to me. What stories do I know? Personal stories hit very close to home.

When I started to date the young woman who would become my wife, I noticed that she was a stickler for driving safely and wearing seatbelts. She had not yet disclosed to me the reason for her insistence. When I visited her home to meet her family, I met her mother and father, her older brother and her younger sister. Pictures of these family members graced the walls of her home, along with pictures of another young man and young woman. I commented that I recognized everyone in the photographs except these final two.

"Who are they?" I asked.

It was a difficult moment.

"This is my brother, Larry, and this is my sister, Wanda."

"Why haven't I met them?"

"They were both killed in automobile accidents."

My heart sank. I had joked earlier in our dating relationship about my wife's overly cautions attitudes about automobile travel. What a weight my wife and her family had been carrying! The very reason I was able to speak light-heartedly earlier was that I, like most college students, had

---

[3]The first two kinds of evidence (or proofs) considered--**facts and statistics--used primarily *logos*** as the means of persuasion. The third proof **(authorities) used primarily *ethos*** as the means of persuasion. The final three proofs--**anecdotes, case studies, and scenarios--primarily employ *pathos* as the means of persuasion.** However, **anecdotes actually use all three,** and *case studies* use two--*pathos* and *logos*.

given little credence to the possibility of being killed in an automobile accident. Now, I was brought face-to-face not only with the reality of such occurrences but also with the devastating emotional and financial effects of such deaths. That my wife and her family were able to cope with not just one, but two such accidents is incredible.

My wife's older sister Wanda had been a student at Purdue University. One evening, she and her boyfriend had been driving his car, just as nighttime began to fall. A truck from a stone quarry near their home was traveling the same road, in the same direction, with a heavy cargo of crushed stone, moving slowly on the highway, at night, without lights. The owners of the truck were conserving on maintenance costs, and had failed to repair the lights. Wanda and her boyfriend came upon the truck from behind. They did not see it until it was too late.

Some months later, my wife's brother Larry--then a student at Indiana State University--was home for a short vacation. He and his church buddies were traveling together on the same two-lane highway on which Wanda had died. An oncoming driver pulled out to pass another car, just as the boys approached from the opposite direction. A head-on collision occurred. Larry and all of his friends were killed.

No one can convince me that college students do not face the problem under consideration. Statistics indicating that only two out of one thousand young people will die in a given year do not mean anything to the families of those two individuals. I have seen the devastation. I have seen the financial crisis that parents face when their college-age children die. My father-in-law earned an excellent income . . . before the crises. His health failed. His financial picture plummeted.

Later, agents whom I contracted told similar stories. Their family members and friends died in plane crashes and motorcycle accidents. Few, if any, proofs of the existence of a problem can match the strength of the *pathos* of a story that affects one personally.

Case Studies

Case studies, like anecdotes, are *true stories*. Yet, a case study is *a story found through research*. The one relating the story *does not have first hand knowledge*. Hence, there is no *ethos* attributable to the one relating a *case study*, such as there is to the one relating an *anecdote*. Nevertheless, since *the case study* is a real life example of the point being made, it **encompasses both** inductive reasoning/*logos* and *pathos*.

As I was considering whether to begin a career marketing life insurance to college seniors and graduate students, the recruiting company supplied several case studies: stories about college seniors and graduate students who had purchased life insurance from the company and subsequently died. Each story told of a family's gratitude that their son or daughter had possessed the wisdom and love to purchase the insurance when they did.

While these case studies were useful, I have always found that newspaper accounts of the recent deaths of students at the specific university where I was selling were much more powerful in persuading myself that the problem exists . . . at this particular campus. For reasons pertaining to the privacy of those families that were affected, I will not recount any specific case studies in this book. But, **newspaper stories** of the tragic deaths of college students, unfortunately, do abound. With internet technology, a simple search of the name of the college or university, the year, and terms such as fatality, student, collision, accidental death, etc. will quickly supply case studies. If I doubt that a problem exists, it does not take too many days of reading the newspaper or too many minutes of **searching the internet** to remove this doubt.

Scenarios

Scenarios are *stories about events that have not actually occurred, but could easily occur*. The stories are fictional, but realistic. As stories, scenarios are able to elicit emotion/*pathos* from the audience. One could argue that, since **anecdotes carry *ethos*, *pathos*, and *logos***, and since **case studies have *pathos* and *logos***, and since **scenarios have only *pathos***, it is always better to use anecdotes or case studies, rather than scenarios for purposes of persuasion. This would be *incorrect*. While scenarios are not true stories and, hence, carry less *logos* and *ethos*, they have **one remarkable attribute** that frequently allows them to be more persuasive than anecdotes or case studies. They *can be adapted to place the audience within the context of the story*!

The use of a scenario to place the audience within the context of the story is actually a very good example of the ways in which Burke's concepts of *identification* and *entelechy* can be applied for persuasive purposes. When a person sees himself/herself living according to a preestablished narrative that has a beginning, middle, and end, the full narrative implicitly shapes the person's present and future actions. This is entelechy. If I offer a scenario with a context into which I have placed my audience, I offer a preestablished narrative with which my audience easily identifies.

I may even offer a **scenario to myself**. At the time I was considering the insurance sales position, I was a graduate student! I wasn't terribly wealthy (to put it mildly). I had a wife and four children. What would happen if the story told was the story of my death?

Just suppose that I am driving home from school. Suppose that an individual driving a semi is coming from the opposite direction. He has been pushing himself, trying to meet a deadline, and is extremely tired . . . but I do not know that. At the moment that I glance down to locate my pocket calendar, the semi driver dozes off momentarily and wanders into my lane of traffic. I look up but it is too late. What would happen then to my wife? My children? How would my death affect my parents?

Since a decision needs to be made whether one will sell/market a specific product, it is easier to make a sound decision if one follows a decision sequence model. According to Paul Copley (2004), a **decision sequence model [DSM]** is a framework for making decisions—a methodology that can be adapted by the one making the decision to a variety of issues in various contexts (p. 75-76). The DSM used in Copley's book is **APIC**. The letters of APIC stand for: **Analysis** of the present situation (situation analysis of company, product, market, and target customer), **Planning** (objectives, positioning, strategy, and tactics), **Implementation** (costing, budgeting, production, and scheduling), and Control (research, monitoring, and evaluation). Although the APIC model is somewhat simpler than the model used in this book, both models begin with analysis and proceed to planning, and eventually to implementation.

The **analysis** with which every marketing plan **begins** relates to *whether there is a need* for the product or service we are marketing. Whether the need is actually a desperate need or merely a desire on the part of some segment of the consuming public (or business entity, in B2B [business to business] marketing), this is **the absolute starting point** for marketing communication. We market only those products and services for which there are potential customers.

Does a problem exist among college seniors and graduate students that cries out for life insurance solutions? I persuaded myself that it does, using all of the available types of evidence-- *facts*, *statistics*, *authorities*, *anecdotes*, *case studies*, and *scenarios*. Looking for a Toulminian **qualifier**, I may use the term "definitely." A problem *definitely* exists.

SALE NUMBER TWO

My Product is a Proper Solution for the Problem

Subject: My product being a proper solution for the need/problem.

Theme: Reasons for my product being a proper solution for the need/problem.

Proposition: My product is a proper solution for the need/problem.

Interrogative: Why?

Key Word: Reasons.

Audience: Self.

Objective: To persuade myself that my product is a proper solution for the need/problem.

Divisions (i.e., "reasons"):

1. My product addresses the cause(s) of the problem

2. My product will solve the problem

3. My product is feasible

Having persuaded myself that a problem/need exists, I turn to the **second sale** that must be made. I must *persuade myself* that *my product is a proper solution* to the problem/need that I have identified. To have *begun* with this sale would be to have "gotten the cart before the horse." I cannot begin to consider a solution until I have identified the problem. To place this sale *later* would be senseless. There is no point in continuing with the twenty-one sales if the product that I would be selling is not a proper solution for the problem.

This sale is made largely through **comparison and contrast**. *If* there were a perfect solution for the need/problem, easily recognized by everyone, *no sale would be necessary.* In reality, usually alternative and competing solutions must be considered. The **objective at this stage is not** necessarily to persuade myself that my product is the *only* solution or even the *best* solution to the problem/need. The **objective is** to persuade myself that my product is *a proper solution* for the need/problem. In order for the solution to be a proper one, it must fit **three criteria**: (1) It must **address the cause** of the problem, (2) It must actually **solve** the problem, and (3) It must be **feasible**.

Before I consider these three criteria, which I have phrased as the reasons my product provides a proper solution for the need/problem, I must **first** honestly **list** all of the potential **alternative solutions** for the problem/need that I can. Using my own personal example, once again, I might list the following solutions to the problem of college seniors and graduate students needing money in the event of their death:

- Leave the problem to your family
- Rely on some religious organization
- Hope that some government agency will come up with the money
- Save up the money in a bank, mutual fund, etc.
- Play the lottery until you win
- Steal the money
- Purchase life insurance from a different company

My Product Addresses the Cause of the Problem

I should clarify, here, that I am **not** persuading myself that my product "**addresses the problem**." This is a confusion that many salespersons encounter at this point. Virtually all solutions "address the problem." I am persuading myself, instead, that my product "addresses the cause of the problem." In order to compare my product with the other possible solutions to the problem, it is necessary to have some idea of **what caused/causes the problem**. What causes seniors and graduate students to need money at the time of their death? I begin with a simple **causal analysis**:

The **first two causes** were mentioned earlier--*final expenses* and *needs of dependents*. These are causes of the variety which Axelrod and Cooper (1994) term "necessary **causes**." *Without these causes, there would be no problem.* They are also "obvious **causes**," *apparent to everyone.* They are are "sufficient **causes**"--they *can cause the problem all by themselves.* While the *needs of dependents* may be a "remote **cause**" (i.e., these expenses may *have been around for some time*), the *final expenses* represent an "immediate **cause**" (i.e., these expenses *come about at precisely the same time as the problem*) (p. 364).

The *specific and individual causes of the death* are *less relevant* to the problem. Even the number one cause of death for this age group (automobile accidents) is no more relevant to the problem than the rarest cause (some previously unknown illness). However, if there is a way to reduce the possibility of death, one should certainly take advantage of it. Nevertheless, **death itself is the greatest cause of the problem**, regardless of how it occurs. Death is an **obvious**, **immediate**, **necessary**, and often **sufficient** cause of the problem (that seniors and graduate students need money).

The **single cause that remains to be added** in order to supply a **fully sufficient cause** of the problem is the *lack of available money.* If sufficient money is available to pay for final expenses and to take care of dependents, the financial problem, at least, is solved.

After completing my causal analysis, I compare my product/solution with other **potential solutions**:

1) *Leaving the problem to one's family* does sometimes *address the cause of the problem, if* the student's family is well-to-do. Yet, *most* college seniors and graduate students at schools in my intended market are *not from wealthy families.* Families to whom these expenses are

insignificant typically send their children to Ivy League or at least private schools, not to state universities. Since most college seniors and graduate students tend to think of themselves as somewhat independent, anyway, they are not inclined to saddle their parents with such expenses. *If the student is married,* it is likely that the financial **problem is exacerbated**. The student and spouse are typically deeply in debt, already. The added expenses of death and caring for dependents would produce a financial nightmare. Leaving the problem to one's family in this situation *does not address the cause of the problem.*

2) *Relying upon religious organizations* may address the cause of the problem for some. Religious people will often help in a time of crisis. But the budget of most religious organizations would be severely compromised if many took advantage of this religious care. If a student truly believes in the work of his/her religious organization, that person might prefer to take care of his/her own financial needs and, thus, relieve the burden on the religious organization.

3) *Government agencies* do, at times, provide an extremely small death benefit, *but* this does not typically apply in the case of the death of a college student. Usually, it is necessary to have paid money into the social security system in order to receive a few hundred dollars at death. College students may not qualify. Those who are military veterans may receive some assistance, but, even here, the family does not always take advantage of the services because there are strict requirements for such benefits. The family may desire more expensive arrangements than any form of government aid can provide.

4) *Saving enough money* may *take too long*. The problem that exists is a current problem. What happens if the student dies today? Saving does not address immediate needs.

5) *Playing the lottery* usually exacerbates the problem. It is much more likely that someone will be in worse financial straits for having played the lottery. This does not address the cause.

6) *Stealing* may actually provide the cause of death! A thief may be shot while attempting to solve his/her financial problems. I think we may safely pass on this option.

7)   *Purchasing life insurance from another company* is really **the only other serious alternative** worth considering. A life insurance policy, even from another company, addresses the cause of the problem by providing cash at the very moment that the cash is needed. Of course, my product produces the same result. Therefore, *my product addresses the <u>cause</u> of the problem*. Although I did not always use the introductory terminology of Toulminian *rebuttals* and *backing* ("*unless*" and "*but*"), I have just conducted **Toulminian analysis** on several possible solutions.

My Product Will Solve the Problem

The second reason my product is a proper solution for the need/problem is that it *will solve the problem*. Here, I may want to review those *case studies* mentioned in **Sale Number One** that *my company supplied*. I prefer to use those case studies, rather than case studies I may find in the newspaper or on the internet, because the company gave them as examples of cases in which *my company's products solved problems*. I want to be certain that my product actually does what it claims to do. I may want to *check with* the Better Business Bureau or other *industry or consumer rating service* to see if there are any complaints against my company's product. Since my case involves an insurance benefit that might not be paid out until several years later, I may want to *investigate the financial stability of my company*. I need to know that this product is guaranteed if unforeseen circumstances cause my company to collapse.

In my case, all of the research produced positive reports. My product has always solved the problem in the past. But, what about the *other alternative solutions*? I want to research these, too, once again using **Toulminian analysis**. *Leaving the problem to the family* does not always work. Most families can not comfortably afford the expenses associated with the death of a child. *Religious organizations and the government* do not always come through. *Saving the money* works only if the student lives long enough to accumulate the cash. There is no guarantee of that. *Playing the lottery* rarely works. *Stealing* is against the law. I would not recommend it, even if it did work. *Purchasing insurance from other companies* works only if students are able to pay the required premiums. If a student cannot continue to pay the premiums, the competitor's policy will lapse. This brings me to the **third reason** my product is a proper solution for the need/problem: My product is feasible.

My Product is Feasible

According to *Webster's*, "**feasible**" refers to *that which is "capable of being done or carried out."* It is feasible to *leave the financial problems to one's family*, but this solution does not usually address the cause of the problem or solve the problem. It is usually not feasible to *rely on religious organizations or the government*. *Saving the money* is not feasible if someone dies today. *Winning the lottery* is not very feasible at all. *Stealing* has low feasibility. And, unfortunately, for college seniors and graduate students, *purchasing life insurance from 99 percent of the insurance companies* in America is not very feasible either. College seniors and graduate students do not typically have sufficient disposable income to afford life insurance premium payments.

This is where my product shines. Not only does my product *address the cause* of the problem and *solve* it, my product is *feasible*! Any college senior or graduate student (graduating within the next twelve months) who is able to qualify for the insurance can obtain a promissory note to pay for the first year's coverage. Once the student graduates and is gainfully employed, s/he begins to make feasible payments. A portion of the payment is earmarked for premium, another portion for the repayment of the promissory note. Since these payments are plugged into the new graduate's budget early, they are feasible once the graduate begins to earn an income.

In **Sale Number One**, I identify a problem which exists, producing a need for my product. I use facts, statistics, authorities, anecdotes, case studies, and scenarios to prove to myself that the problem exists. In **Sale Number Two**, I offer three reasons my product is a proper solution for the problem/need that I identified: (1) My product addresses the cause(s) of the problem, (2) My product will solve the problem, and (3) My product is feasible. **These are the same three**

reasons a person who sells any product should provide in order to be persuaded that his/her product is a proper solution for the problem/need which s/he has identified.

Marketing (as distinguished from "marketing communication") is concerned primarily with what have been called **"the Four P's"** of Marketing:

1. **Product** (Will market demand support the development and sale of our proposed product? Is our product needed? Is our product competitive enough to compete in the marketplace?)

2. **Placement** (Where will our product be made available? Where will we sell it? How will it be delivered? Do we have a means of distributing our product?)

3. **Promotion** (The way Marketing uses the term "Promotion" is as a synonym for what we are calling "Marketing Communication." Hence, by the term "Promotion," Marketing refers to Advertising, Public Relations, Personal Sales, Promotions, Packaging, Sponsorships, Direct Marketing, Online Marketing, Diffusion of Innovations, Mobile Marketing), and

4. **Price** (What must we or should we charge for our product or service? Can we afford to sell our product or service at competitive rates?)

In **Sale Number Two**, I am only concerned with the first "P" of Marketing: **Product**. I must persuade myself that **my product** is a proper solution for the problem/need that I identified. If I am persuaded that it is **not**, I should stop this process in its tracks. There is no point in continuing to **Sale Number Three**, if I do not believe that my product is a proper solution for the problem/need that I identified.

.

SALE NUMBER THREE

I am the Right Person to Sell This Solution

Subject: My being the right person to sell this solution.

Theme: Reasons for my being the right person to sell this solution.

Proposition: I am the right person to sell this solution.

Interrogative: Why?

Key Word: Reasons.

Audience: Self.

Objective: To persuade myself that I am the right person to sell this solution.

Divisions (i.e., "reasons"):

1. I have enough product knowledge

2. I have enough communicative skill

3. I have had enough practice at persuading

4. I am able to philosophically handle negatives

Very well! I have persuaded myself that there is a need for my product and my product is a proper solution for the need. Does that mean **that I should be a marketer of this product**? Not necessarily. Just as not everybody has the specific need that calls for my product and not every proposed solution or product is the proper solution for a given need, so **not every person is the right person to sell a given solution**.

At the time my prospective company was recruiting me as an agent (salesperson) they promised to place me on a fast-track to becoming a general agent (manager). I would certainly want to prove to myself that I could sell my product before I recruited people into the business. This was a matter of **ethics** for me. If I could not sell the product, I did not feel ethical in hiring others and asking them to sell the product. On the other hand, I thought that if I could be successful in selling, **I could teach others to sell just as I had sold**. As you might surmise, I did decide to pursue this particular sales career. Later, when the general agent contract was actually awarded to me, I had been successful in one year of sales. To find employees, I placed advertisements, conducted interviews, and contracted agents. My first year as a manager was financially successful, but **not primarily because I was able to help my agents succeed**. I learned very quickly that I had overlooked an extremely important sale in the twenty-one sales. My agents had sold themselves that the need existed and that the product was a proper solution, as I had sold myself on these propositions. But, **they had not sold themselves** on the proposition **that they were the right persons to sell the product**.

Essentially, there are four **reasons** why **someone is the right person to sell a given solution**:

1. S/he has enough **product knowledge**.
2. S/he has enough **communicative skill**.
3. S/he has had enough **practice at persuading**.
4. S/he is **able to philosophically handle negatives**.

Whether I sell life insurance, shoes, or donut holes, I need to be able to claim that these four reasons apply to me.

I Have Enough Product Knowledge

The first reason that I am the right person to sell this solution is that I have enough product knowledge--I know enough about the product and the problem that it solves to credibly discuss these matters with prospects. In other words, I have *ethos*--at least the expertise side of it. It is very arguable that the **active goodwill** side of *ethos* also requires that I know what I am talking about. Is it possible, for example, for a physician to have active goodwill towards his/her patient, if the physician gives a patient advice on an illness that the physician knows little about? When, in the Introduction, I speak of **competence stress**, I define it as "the stress one feels when one questions one's own competence to perform a task." I further suggest that "[t]his stress may be due to a lack of self-esteem, a lack of knowledge on the subject, or a lack of . . . skill, etc." While, in the Introduction, I am actually discussing the **stress that a prospect might be feeling**, the very **same stress** may be **felt by the salesperson**. You should **not** begin selling to others until you make **Sale Number Three** to yourself.

In my case, it was necessary for me to be *licensed* before I could sell, anyway. I needed to *study insurance law* and *product design* **before** I was *allowed to sell*. Furthermore, my company flew me to Texas for a special *week of intensive product training* before I began my career. I did not have as much expertise as a seasoned professional in the insurance business, but I did possess enough product knowledge to credibly discuss matters with prospects. By the time I was contracting agents, however, company policy had changed. The company wanted new agents to make five sales before receiving the company-paid week of intensive product training. A couple of my agents did not make it that far. Nevertheless, all of my agents were licensed before beginning to sell, so they possessed some product knowledge.

If the salesperson is not yet able to claim this reason, all is not lost. The **remedy is study**. The salesperson must study the product intensively until s/he thoroughly knows the product and the problem that it solves.

If the salesperson is *unwilling or unable* to thoroughly understand these matters, **this sale has not been made**, and there is no point in continuing with the twenty-one sales. The individual is *NOT* the right person to sell this solution. To send a salesperson who does not have product knowledge out to a prospect is **unethical**. Furthermore, this is not a sale that a recruiter can make to a salesperson. **You must convince yourself** that you want this sale enough to study to achieve it.

I Have Enough Communicative Skill

Assuming, however, that you have been able to persuade yourself that you have enough product knowledge, the **second reason** you are the right person to sell this solution is that *you have enough communicative skill to adequately teach and persuade prospects.* Let's face it. Not everyone has **communicative skill**. One of the agents whom I contracted had tremendous product knowledge. He had earned a perfect grade point average in college. His major was accounting, which was perfect for financial consulting. The dream agent, right? Wrong.

The agent stuttered. He would pick up the phone to call a prospect. The prospect would answer. The agent would begin: "H-h-h-h-hello. Th-th-this is K-k-k-keith w-w-w-w-with th-the C-c-c-college B-b-b-benefit P-p-pr-program . . . ." The other person on the line would hang up. Believe it or not, Keith made several sales, but it was clear that this was not the best career for a person with his skills and credentials. He did possess credentials on paper but lacked speaking skills.

On the other hand, some salespersons whom others might reject outright, I would definitely contract. Some people are shy. They lack self-confidence in the communication department. This can be remedied. *Shyness is* little more than *a competence stress.* In order to remedy shyness, the individual needs to possess product knowledge and communication skill, and to engage in some **practice** at communicating and persuading.

I am shy in many contexts, but that does not mean that I am not the right person to sell my solution. I have communication skills. I was probably the shyest boy in my high school graduating class, but I won two state championships and one world championship in public speaking. I studied hard to improve my communication skill. I completed the coursework for two Ph.D. degrees in communication. This does not mean that I am aggressive at mingling—I am not—but give me an audience (whether it is a crowd or a single individual) and I can be quite persuasive.

You need not pursue a Ph.D. in communication in order to claim that you have enough communicative skill to adequately teach and persuade prospects. **Studying the book that you have in your hands** should help you to make the claim. The book distills the most important persuasive principles from two Ph.D. programs worth of coursework and helps you apply them to your specific situation.

I Have Had Enough Practice at Persuading

The old maxim, "Practice makes perfect," is true. You may have product knowledge and know how persuasion is accomplished, but, in the final analysis, there is no substitute for practice.

You learned this point when overcoming the **competence stress of learning** to drive a car. Even though, as a prospective driver, you may have aced the written test covering the rules of the road, even though you may have aced all the written exams in Drivers Education, you may have been extremely tense sitting behind the wheel for the first time. Your hands may have gripped the steering wheel at the ten o'clock and two o'clock position so tightly that your knuckles may have turned white. Your foot may have alternated swiftly between the accelerator and the brake. The muscles in your neck and upper back may have been tight as you sat erect in the driver's seat.

But, after several years of driving, you may slump lazily in the seat, handling the wheel with one hand, trying to stay awake and alert despite the boredom. What has happened? Practice. There is no longer any competence stress. You know how to drive and have had plenty of **practice**.

The very same principle works in sales. It may seem rough at first, but gradually you learn to ease back in your seat and let practiced instincts take control. The more relaxed you are, the more relaxed will be your prospect. Amazingly, self-confidence and relaxation add to your *ethos*. Prospects are much more likely to trust someone who seems relaxed and comfortable than someone who is tense and who stumbles through the presentation. Before you are ready to go out on that first sales interview, you must be able to tell yourself, "I have had enough practice at persuading." If you cannot yet claim this reason, the remedy is easy: Practice more! You will quickly become competent. In my book (2004, p. 89-91), I cite Sprague and Stuart (2000) in listing the **four stages in developing competence**:

The **first stage** is **unconscious incompetence**. "In this stage a person is not aware that he or she is making errors in some area, and may even be unaware that there is a skill to be learned" (Sprague 14). Babies are at this stage in communication skills. You could also call this stage naïveté. [A] boring man . . . might not even realize that conversation is a skill that can be learned. When I coached elementary school basketball players, it was easy to see that they were at this stage with regard to basketball skills. There is very little competence stress here. This explains why some people may be stress-free at first, then develop competence stress later.

The **second stage** is **conscious incompetence**. "A person at this stage has made the realization that she or he is doing something ineptly and that there is room for improvement. In many cases this awareness creates anxiety, which actually increases incompetence" (Sprague 14). How do you learn that you are incompetent? Perhaps someone mentioned it to you or perhaps you observed the fact as you compared yourself to others. This is the **increasing stage in competence stress**, but it is not necessarily a bad thing. It has been said that nobody likes criticism. While that may be true, most of us can benefit from it. We do not like it partly because it increases our competence stress. . . . Nevertheless, as you enter the stage of conscious incompetence, you should expect your competence stress levels to rise. You are discovering new areas in which you are not fully competent. This is somewhat stressful, but handle the stress with humility. You know that you need improvement in these areas and you are determined to prepare and practice until you improve.

The **third stage** of developing competence is **conscious competence**. According to Sprague and Stuart, "In this stage a person has taken a skill in which she or he feels incompetent, has improved, and then devotes a portion of consciousness to performing it competently. . . . [I]f a person perseveres, the awkwardness of the new behavior diminishes and the need for self-monitoring lessens" (Sprague 14). As you enter the stage of conscious competence, you should expect **your competence stress levels to decrease**. The stress is not completely absent, but you know you can be competent so long as you devote some attention to what you are doing. With reference to my driving example, . . . this is the stage at which you are a *competent driver, but* you still must keep your hands at the ten o'clock and two o'clock position. You must always keep your eyes on the road. You will not allow other activities such as eating, talking on the phone, or perhaps even conversing or listening to the radio to distract you. You are competent, but you are still experiencing competence stress.

The **fourth** and final **stage** of developing competence [is] **unconscious competence**. You are good at what you do and you know it. You feel very little competence stress whatsoever.

I Am Able to Philosophically Handle Negatives

This is usually the kicker. Individuals who are otherwise extremely qualified salespersons have been stopped in their tracks by the negatives inherent in a sales career. You should ask yourself such questions as:

- Am I the type of person who would ask someone for a date, even if I knew that the answer might very well be no?

- Would I run for an office (in school, church, government, etc.) if I thought I might lose?

- Would I put myself in a situation in which I knew I could be criticized?

- Would I be able to respond calmly if I were fired from a job?

- Am I able to go on with my life, positively, even when I have lost at sports or love or at a job promotion or in an argument or in a class at school?

The point is: Do you have enough **self-esteem** to maintain a feeling of self-worth even *if you are told "no" on a highly regular basis*? The fact is, as a salesperson, **you will be**. Sometimes you will be told "no" because you have found a prospect who does not have a problem. Sometimes you will be told "no" because your prospect actually has found a better solution to the problem. But, usually, this is not the case. Usually, you will be told "no" because your prospect believes he is too busy to pay attention, she believes the matter is not relevant to her, he doubts your legitimacy, she believes the information that you wish to provide will not be worth her time to consider, he does not believe there is a problem, she does not believe that you are qualified to help her, he does not believe you have a proposal that is worth considering, she does not want to make a decision, etc. **These are some of the upcoming interpersonal sales that I discuss** in the book. My goal is to help you as a salesperson avoid some "no's" in these parts of the sales process, but **the only guaranteed way to completely eliminate "no's" is to stop selling**.

At one time, I gave a traveling trophy each week to the salesperson in my agency who took the most "no's" for the week. I reasoned that the person who received the most "no's" would usually also receive the most "yes's." Generally, that was true, but somehow the practice always seemed to be a negative way to make my point, and eventually I discontinued it. I did not want to encourage people to continue to receive "no's" when by working to improve their twenty-one sales, they could minimize the number of negative responses. I wanted to celebrate "yes's" instead.

Before I became a salesperson, I spent several years in a career in which I was constantly bombarded with criticism. As with the negatives of sales, some of the feedback was justified, but most of it was not. In talking to others in the same career, I discovered that I was not alone. Apparently, criticism goes with the territory. I learned to take it, smile, and politely move on. This actually was a **good preparation for sales**, and, for that matter, a good preparation for life. I learned that I believed in myself despite the negatives. So, when a prospect later told me "no," I took it, smiled, and politely moved on.

I (humbly) believe that I am better qualified to determine whether someone needs my product than s/he is. **If someone honestly does not need my product, I tell him/her so**. However, some life insurance salespersons have made careers out of **replacing insurance policies** that are already in force. This is **rarely in the client's interest**. The way the replacement sale is typically made involves **incomplete disclosure on the part of the salesperson**. I think this is **unethical**. I believe that the client is entitled to know the *advantages of keeping the old policy*. I believe that the client needs to know *how to best use the provisions of the old policy*. I may recommend additional coverage, but **I avoid replacing policies that are viable**. There have been times when one of my clients has decided to replace the policy that I sold him/her with a different policy from a new agent. This amounts to a negative. But, **I know, and probably the other agent knows, that the client has made a stupid mistake**. This does not stop me from recommending my solution to others.

Let me put it another way. When I was single, and in college, I (humbly) believed that I was a great catch. If I asked a woman for a date and she told me "no," I knew that she had made a stupid mistake. This did not stop me from asking other women for dates.

This is **how we philosophically handle negatives**. We must **know our product** and the **details of the problem** which that product solves. We must know **how to communicate** and persuade. We must **practice** and enhance our skills. And, if it seems that the prospect has made a stupid mistake by saying "no," we must *chalk it up to the stupidity of the prospect, and not take it personally*. This must not stop us from offering the product to others.

Kenneth Burke (1943 and 1969) offers a **grammar of motives** that features the five terms of his **Pentad: Scene, Act, Agent, Agency**, and **Purpose**. As applied to the sales process, we may be motivated by any of these five terms. Our **Purpose** may be as noble as "uniting consumers with products that will make their lives happier" or as ignoble as "squeezing every dime of commission we can get out of every prospect." The **Scene** that motivates us may be "an overtaxed economy that cries out for tax-sheltering strategies" or "cold climates that cry out for warm clothing and efficient heating systems." The **Act** in which we are engaged is "selling products," not "scamming the unsuspecting or naïve." The **Agencies** we use may be the telephone, the computer screen, charts and diagrams, models, (demonstrating) the actual product, high pressure techniques or soft-sale techniques, psychology, *ethos*, *pathos*, *logos*, etc.

However, this chapter focuses on you as the **Agent**. Assuming that you meet the requirements for selling a specific product (set forth in this chapter), what exists in **you** that motivates you to seel a specific product or service? Let's say you are a dedicated Republican or Democrat. If your political view represents your reason for existence, you may be internally motivated to convert others to your political party (the sale) simply because that is the kind of person you are. That would be a motivation based upon you as the **Agent**. If your mother died of breast cancer, you as an **Agent** may be internally motivated to raise funds to find a cure (the sale) because you love your mother so much that you want to defeat the evil that took her life. If you love to travel, you may be internally motivated as an **Agent** to sell cruises, travel services, resort condominium time-shares, etc. If you are athletically-inclined, you may be motivated as an **Agent** to sell exercise equipment, tickets to sporting events, sports memorabilia, etc.

While most individuals may be motivated by making money, that is an **external motivation**, as opposed to the **internal motivations** mentioned earlier—those that stemmed from your nature as an Agent. In order to be a good salesperson, there should be some internal characteristic you possess that screams out the particular product or service you would be selling. Otherwise, you may be only externally motivated. In my case, I chose to sell life insurance products to college students. **I was internally motivated** by the untimely deaths of my wife's brother and sister— two college students—Larry and Wanda, to whom I have dedicated this book.

In 1979, I was ready to become a salesperson. I had convinced myself that a problem existed and that my product was a proper solution for the problem. I had convinced myself that I was the right person to sell the solution. Why? Because I possessed plenty of product knowledge, I was a skillful communicator, I had practiced and enhanced my skill, and I was able to philosophically handle the negatives. As an Agent, I was internally motivated. I was ready for the next sale.

SALE NUMBER FOUR

I Should Do Market Research

Subject: Doing market research.

Theme: Reasons for doing market research.

Proposition: I should do market research.

Interrogative: Why?

Key Word: Reasons.

Audience: Self.

Objective: To persuade myself that I should do market research.

Divisions (i.e., "reasons"):

1. Doing market research eliminates a lot of negatives

2. Doing market research provides superior time management

3. Doing market research increases income

4. Doing market research makes me more knowledgeable about my prospects

5. Doing market research allows me to help those who need help the most

Doing research sounds boring to many individuals. They see research as something like locking themselves up in a laboratory or a dusty library where they must concern themselves with unending statistics and interminable reading. Therefore, many would-be salespersons **skip this sale . . . to their detriment**. A sales proverb that caught my attention early in my career was:

"**Work smart, not hard**." It certainly is hard work to carry a refrigerator, loaded with food, from the truck into the kitchen. It is smarter to carry the food in first, then transport the empty refrigerator. It is smarter still to use a hand truck, a tool that is designed to make the work easier, to transport the refrigerator. It may take a few minutes to locate a hand truck, but it makes for much smarter work.

A **market** can be understood to be the **location or region** where products and services are bought and sold (such as my *locations*—Purdue University, Indiana State University, Ball State University, the University of Illinois, and Illinois State University) or it can be understood as a particular **category of buyer** (such as my categories (college seniors and graduate students within 12 months of graduating). **Market research** is is research (about a **product** such as life insurance being offered by one's competitors, the **specific characteristics of individuals fitting in the category of buyer** in the target market, etc.) used to gather information about a particular market. Market research, in sales, includes (among other things) determining which geographical area you will be serving, finding out what kind of potential selling opportunities exist in that market for your product or service, understanding consumer desires and needs (and who is competing with you in that market), and discovering who will make decisions.

Like using a hand truck to move a refrigerator, **market research is designed to make sales work smarter and easier**. Keep in mind that there are **three basic kinds of research**. **Laboratory research** is *one* kind that the typical salesperson will not engage in. However, some results of laboratory research may be quite helpful to the salesperson. **Library research** is the *second* kind. Studying Aristotle, Toulmin, and Burke involves library research. The *third* type of research is **field research**, which primarily involves conducting interviews and questionnaires and making personal, on-site observations. Consider the **research steps** through which you are proceding:

- **Sale Number One** requires some **evidentiary research**. You must dig for *facts, statistics, authorities, anecdotes, case studies*, and *scenarios* in order to persuade yourself that **there**

really is a need for the product in question (a problem). This research is often *library* research (although, these days, much of the search for the information may be completed on the *internet*). If you conclude that there really *is not* a need for the product, you have **worked smart**, and **will not waste time** gaining product knowledge concerning a product that is unnecessary. If you eliminate a specific problem to solve, but still want to be a salesperson, you might consult a book such as Nancy Drescher's *Which business? Help in selecting your new venture* (1997), which is a compendium of 24 real business opportunities. In other words, you might continue to **do further research until you find a legitimate need for which products exist**.

- If you discover a need for which a product does not exist, and **you have a creative idea** for a product that might be a proper solution for that need, you might consult a step-by-step manual that outlines all of the stages of **new product development**, such as *Develop and market your creative ideas* by Dale A. Davis (1996). This is **product development research**.

- Once the research has satisfactorily produced a need and a proper solution (product), you must research to **gain product knowledge** and **sales/persuasion expertise**. This is **product knowledge research** and **persuasion skill research**.

- Then, if you are truly smart, you will do **market research**. There are **five basic reasons** for **doing market research**:

  1. Doing market research **eliminates a lot of negatives**.
  2. Doing market research provides **superior time management**.
  3. Doing market research **increases income**.
  4. Doing market research **makes you more knowledgeable** about your prospects.
  5. Doing market research **allows you to help those who need** help the most.

Let's consider these reasons, one at a time.

Doing Market Research Eliminates a Lot of Negatives

In **Sale Number Three**, I point out your need to be able to handle **negatives** philosophically. I certainly stand by my earlier assertions, but I *do not recommend that you be a glutton for punishment*. No human desires to hear negatives, so why should you face more negatives than are necessary? The advice offered in each of the twenty-one sales in this book is designed to produce positives, not negatives. And, so it is with my advice in **Sale Number Four**. I realize that **I am inclined to tell myself "no," when it comes to this sale** as well as **Sale Number Five**. **In these two sales** (and **nowhere else**), I urge you as a salesperson to get pushy. **Do not take "no" for an answer! You are your own audience here. You should determine not to let yourself off the hook!**

Rather than have a prospect tell you, "No, I do not need my roof repaired; I rent this house," you should do research to determine who the homeowners are. Rather than have a prospect tell you, "No, I cannot afford a new car; I am unemployed," you should conduct a preliminary (telephone?) interview with the prospect to determine the feasibility of the sale. Rather than have a prospect explain, "No, I cannot qualify to purchase a $200,000.00 home; I make only $25,000 per year," you should research such matters in advance.

Doing Market Research Provides Superior Time Management

Not only will doing market research eliminate some negatives, it will also **save you valuable time**. The biggest drawback that I experienced in my insurance sales career was the time constraint. I contracted with telephone secretaries to schedule my appointments. I did my research at times that were inappropriate for sales appointments. But, those precious **daily hours** that are set aside **for sales appointments cannot be wasted**. Besides, there is nothing more frustrating than spending an hour with a prospect only to find out that the prospect was not qualified for or did not need my product--especially **if this information** was something that **could have been researched in advance**! I learned very quickly the value of prequalifying my prospects. This **prequalifying** takes several forms.

Before I call an individual on the phone (or have my secretary call), I check the student telephone directory at the university. This directory indicates how many semesters the student has been in college. I call those who have been in college at least six or seven semesters.

When I contact them by phone, I ask when the specific student will be graduating. If the expected graduation date is more than 12 months away, I thank the student for his/her time, and indicate that I will call back when the graduation date is nearer. Students more than 12 months from graduating do not qualify for the company's promissory note.

At first, I scheduled *full interviews* with those who were qualified. Then, since I had more interviews scheduled than I could handle, I put some of the *preliminary sales on video*, so that I could conduct some of the *later sales* with one prospect while other prospects were viewing the *earlier sales*. Later, I put these preliminary sales on an audio recording and mailed it to the prospect. This way, if I failed to make the preliminary sales, I would not waste my scheduled appointment time. Superior time management is a strong reason to do market research.

Doing Market Research Increases Income

Clearly, if your appointment time is spent with prequalified prospects, your chances of making sales are increased; thus, your number of sales increase and your income increases. This is a reason with which I do not need to spend much time, but it is generally a most compelling reason of all for salespersons, especially since we all succumb to some external motivation—the paycheck.

Doing Market Research Makes Me More Knowledgeable About My Prospects

If you am persuaded that you can make more sales by eliminating many unqualified prospects, you might make even more sales if **you know your prospects more thoroughly**. When researching in the student directory the number of semesters the college student had completed, I also noted the student's *major*. I have found that students majoring in engineering have the need for larger amounts of insurance than those majoring in elementary education. There are also certain majors that will command fuller company benefit packages upon employment. I need to know what my clients are likely to receive from work. My goal is not only to sell a product but also to serve a client.

Ethos results not only from **expertise**, but also from **active goodwill**. If I want my prospect to trust me, the prospect needs to know that *I would not intentionally sell her/him something that his/her company will more properly provide*. Hence, I rarely sell permanent health insurance to college seniors and graduate students. I frequently advise them to continue their coverage on their parents' policies as long as possible. I tell them when their coverage will cease (sometimes, upon graduation), and advise the purchase of policies for those months between the cessation of their coverage under their parents' policies and the beginning of their company benefits.

By knowing the prospect's major, fraternity/sorority affiliation, and/or any other piece of personal data in advance, I have **implicitly communicated that I am interested in the prospect as an individual**, not just a sale. I may also have other clients who have the same major or who live in the same "house." These may provide additional *ethos*. My prospect may contact these clients for a personal reference (see **Sale Number Twenty-One**). At the very least, I am able to demonstrate that others whom they know have trusted me.

Doing Market Research Allows Me to Help Those Who Need Help the Most

Those who view sales only as a means of earning income are missing much of the joy that comes from being a salesperson. Like a teacher who only cares about a paycheck, or a social worker who refuses to help indigents, or a doctor who turns away the sick because they have no money, the salesperson who only sells for income does not see the big picture. Of course, I like it when people buy their life insurance from me, but one of the instances of greatest personal satisfaction to me in my sales career was an instance in which I did not make a sale.

The man was a friend of mine. We went to the same church. His older children were the age of my older children. At a relatively young age, he was diagnosed with cancer. I went to the hospital to visit him. I prayed with him. I visited him at home.

It began to appear more and more likely that he was not going to be able to defeat the cancer, and I was told that his wife was planning on going back to school very quickly so she would be able to support herself, and their several children, if he did not make it. I went to see him and asked about his life insurance. He had a small policy, but most of his insurance was through his employer and he was about to be removed from employee status because of his illness. When he left the company's employ, his benefits would cease. I told him that he could continue the coverage by following several steps. Together, we searched his files for any guaranteed insurability options, any and every possible means of providing life insurance proceeds for his family, if he died. **There were no commissions to be made**. **He could not have qualified** for any insurance that I might have tried to sell him. My help was a service of **love**.

When he died, his widow and children were well taken care of. I spoke at his funeral. I reminisced about the rivalry between his favorite university and mine. I missed him. But there was a certain **peace of mind** that came from knowing that I had **helped** my friend and his family. **I would not have been able to help him if** I had not been willing to *see a need*, if I had not *studied to gain the product knowledge necessary to find solutions* in such situations, and if I had not *had the self-confidence to believe that I was the right person to suggest the best solution* for him.

Every year, statistically, nearly **two out of every thousand college seniors and graduate students die**. That translates to 12 out of the graduating class of most major state universities, every year. My job, as I saw it, was to conduct the **research needed to find those whom I could help**. I had a unique product that could offer help to a very specific group of individuals. Market research helped me to identify those whom I could actually help the most. Among this group, it helped me identify those who needed the most help. By allowing me to spend my interviewing time with those who needed the help and those who qualified for the help I could provide, market research helped me make more sales to more people who needed help than I could have accomplished otherwise.

Before you make the first phone call to a phone prospect, you need to **sell yourself on the proposition: I should do market research**. Like some of the prospects you will later encounter, the audience **(that is, you) will want to say no**. But you must persuade yourself that it must be done. This salesperson **(you) must not let this audience (yourself) off the hook**.[4]

---

[4]My objective in this sale is not to inform you concerning how market research is performed. My objective in this sale is to persuade you that you should do market research. For information regarding how it is performed, you should consult books such as David B. Frigstad's *Know your market: How to do low-cost market research* (1994) or Jay Newberg and Claudio Marcus's *TargetSmart! Database marketing for the small business* (1996).

SALE NUMBER FIVE

I Should Call My Prospects

Subject: Calling my prospects.

Theme: Reasons for calling my prospects.

Proposition: I should call my prospects.

Interrogative: Why?

Key Word: Reasons.

Audience: Self.

Objective: To persuade myself that I should call my prospects.

Divisions (i.e., "reasons"):

1. My fear of rejection means that I am taking personally what is essentially impersonal

2. My fear of being incompetent is unfounded

3. My fear of others' rudeness might otherwise let rudeness win

4. Sometimes "stress" is good

5. If I don't call my prospects, I will make no money

My best friend joined me in the life insurance business the year I became a general agent. Actually, I had wanted him to join me long before my opportunity to be a general agent came up. I had been trying to sell him on the career partly because I thought it would be great if he and his wife and their kids lived closer to my family and me, especially if he and I worked together. As it was, we lived two hours from each other. At first, the plan was for him to join me as a fellow agent. We would both sell insurance under the supervision of another general agent/manager. Then, the company offered me a general agent/manager position. My friend joined me as an agent in my new agency.

I really wanted him to be a huge success in the business, not primarily because it would help me be successful as a general agent, but, first, because he was my friend and, second, if he were successful, our families could be reunited.

My friend **easily made the first four "Sales in a Sale" to himself**. He was convinced that *there was a need for our insurance*. Not only did he know the facts, statistics, and authorities, but *he knew personally that college students sometimes lose their lives*. His brother had been the manager for the intercollegiate basketball team at an important university. The entire team was flying to a game on a chartered plane. The plane went down. All aboard were killed. My friend knew from personal experience what the family goes through when a college student in the family dies. He was *internally motivated*.

My friend was persuaded that our *product was a proper solution* for the problem. His brother-in-law and a mutual friend of ours both sold insurance. He knew about their products and he also knew that, in the college market, the *product that we sold was the number one choice* of seniors and graduate students for the reasons I earlier recounted.

He was sold on the idea that *he was the right person to sell the solution*. He became licensed, took the week-long intensive course provided by the company, and knew his product. He had excellent communication skill and was practiced and comfortable in an interview. He thought he would be okay with the negatives involved in sales, **but the phone negatives were his Achilles heel**. He *did the necessary market research*, but the telephone calls became an increasing anathema to him.

I asked him **why** he didn't like making phone calls. It came down to one word: **fear**. I don't know that most people are acutely aware of the phenomenon **phone phobia**, but my friend had it. Many would-be salespersons have it. *What fears or phobias do telephones engender?*

I recall having **phone phobia as an adolescent**. I wanted to call a certain young woman. I was afraid, however, that I would get her on the phone and then not know what to say. This was a communication anxiety, or what I call in my (2004) book, *The seven C's of stress*, a type of competence stress. I **felt incompetent** at conversing with young women on the phone.

Some **elderly** individuals experience **phone phobia** when calling computerized answering systems. They also have a *form of competence stress*. They **feel incompetent** when dealing with the latest types of communication technology. I offer these examples of phone phobia to show that the phenomenon exists, not because the examples were representative of my friend's specific problem. He was neither worried about calling young women nor reaching electronic answering systems.

He simply was afraid of the <u>negatives</u> he might encounter when he called the phone prospect. He knew what he was going to say on the phone. He had practiced it many times. He had no competence stress to speak of. His phobia pertained to the *rudeness* which he might encounter and to a fear of *being rejected*. He needed some good reasons for calling his prospects. I have found **five good reasons for calling** my prospects. Let's consider the first reason.

My Fear of Rejection Means that I Am Taking *Personally* What is Essentially *Impersonal*

One of my friend's fears is related to a phobia similar to my *adolescent* fear of talking to young women on the phone. A young man might be afraid to call a young woman to ask for a date for *fear that she would tell him no*. His fear is **the fear of rejection**. Because of this fear, a lot of **strategizing** usually occurs before a date is requested. Those who plan to ask use strategies to determine in advance what the likely reply will be.

There are some **similarities** between the fear that a salesperson faces and the fear of rejection that is experienced when asking for a date. Certainly, the caller is **asking for a specific date and time** when two people will be getting together. Certainly, **the encounter that is being planned is dyadic** (involving two people). Certainly, the one proposing the get-together is **at risk of being told no**.

Yet, there are also some very important **differences** between these two types of telephone encounters. The sales encounter **has little to do with the desirability of either person as a friend**. The sales encounter is one of thousands of sales encounters; whereas, the date has the potential of being a special encounter. The *date request betrays the caller's personal attraction* to the one being called. If the one being called says no, there is an implicit message: "Clearly, you believe that *I* am attractive, but I do not find *you* attractive." Therefore, the *date request* is **highly personal**. *Not so* with the *request for a sales appointment*. Individuals who find me stimulating on a social basis may actually respond negatively to my offer for a sales appointment. They may respond in this manner *precisely because they value me as a friend* and personally fear that our friendship may be compromised and confused if we did business together.

What happens to too many salespersons is that they **get themselves caught in a dating or friendship entelechy while doing business**. They see themselves calling to ask for a date, not a sales appointment. They are taking personally what is essentially **impersonal**. This is not to say that the sales appointments which result should be unfriendly or impersonal. As Gerald R. Baron recommends in his book, *Friendship marketing: Growing your business by cultivating strategic relationships* (1997), businesses need to slow down on their feeding frenzy approach and work to build profitable and worthwhile relationships. Today's business world is too cut-throat.

In the final analysis, though, **a business relationship is not the same as a friendship**. The satisfaction that is found in a business relationship is not the satisfaction of meeting another human who is a soul-mate. Business offers **the satisfaction of solving a problem**, filling a need. It may be that two people who do business together will become very close friends as well, but that relationship is a separate, social relationship. When I call an individual to ask for an appointment, typically, that individual does not even know me. If that person interprets my request for an appointment as a date request--"I find you attractive, do you find me attractive?"--I have a problem on my hands.

As you will see in the sales in **Part Two** of this book, what is to be accomplished on the phone is "impersonal." These sales are:

- You should give me just one minute of your time
- This matter is relevant to you
- I am/we are a legitimate enterprise
- It is worthwhile for you to consider more information on this subject

There is no sale on the phone that refers to my personal attractiveness. Hence, **these are impersonal sales**. The salesperson must not take personally what is essentially an impersonal encounter.

My Fear of Being Incompetent is Unfounded

The second reason I should call my prospects is that my fear of being incompetent is unfounded. Most salespersons know exactly what they are going to say when they get on the phone. Granted, some who are new to the process may need to refer to some canned answers to objections along the way, but this is hardly similar to the phone phobia that I experienced as an adolescent when calling a young woman. I did not feel competent at making the conversation move along. Here, **the key is editing the conversation so that I can make it as brief as possible while squeezing in four sales**.

Any fear I had of being incompetent as a salesperson was unfounded. As proof of this fact, I was able, later in my career, to contract telephone secretaries whose job it was to make the phone calls and accomplish the four persuasion objectives that comprise **Part Two**. They were given some of the results of my market research--at least, the names and phone numbers and anticipated graduation dates of the students whom they were to call. They were told basically what to say on the phone. They were able to accomplish their tasks quite well. If a telephone secretary could do this task with nothing more than a script and a list of phone numbers, **competence was not the issue** for trained salespersons (except, perhaps, for Keith).

My Fear of Others' Rudeness Might Otherwise Let Rudeness Win

The third reason I should call my prospects has to do with the fear of rudeness. There is no doubt about it, despite my best efforts, I **will encounter rude people on the phone**. Some will justify their rudeness by suggesting that I am rude to call them on the phone. What they usually mean by this comment is that **they have had too many rude telephone solicitors call them before** I did. Many of these solicitors *kept them on the phone for several minutes*. The solicitors *made misleading statements* that were only explained after several minutes. *If the solicitor was told, "No*, thank you," the solicitor came up with a canned line and *proceeded with the pitch*. The prospects discovered that the **only way to get off the phone with these people is to be rude themselves**.

Since I have encountered such rude telephone solicitors, myself, **I can empathize** with the phone prospects. I suggest that salespersons **use the Golden Rule**: "Do unto others as you would have them do unto you." Generally speaking, people who are totally opposed to receiving telephone calls from all but a select few individuals have *unlisted numbers* or *scrupulously use Caller ID*. People who have a real problem with receiving phone calls at specific times such as mealtimes, etc., use voicemail to screen their calls. If the prospects have not gone to such measures to eliminate phone calls, they probably are not opposed to receiving some sales-related telephone inquiries, so long as the salesperson is *considerate*.

Being considerate involves **courtesies** such as:

- Asking, "Have I called at a bad time?"
- Keeping the phone call brief

- Taking "no" for an answer
- Not using misleading statements which must later be explained away
- Using a polite tone

In short, *being considerate* means that **you will not treat someone in a way that you would not appreciate being treated yourself**.

As a salesperson on the phone, you are in a position to *change the expectations* of those whom you have called. They may have *automatically placed you within an inconsiderate telephone solicitor entelechy.* You need to **change that entelechy** to *a considerate business person entelechy*. **If there are no considerate people who use the phone, then rudeness wins.** If you are treated rudely from the very moment you call, clearly the person whom you have called is taking out his/her frustrations from dealing with other callers. Rather than allow this to affect your self-image (or even to assume that the one whom you have called is a jerk), you might simply *blame it on those rude and/or inconsiderate telephone solicitors who spoke to the person before you did*. You must not be rude in return. To do so would be to let rudeness win.

Sometimes Stress is Good

As I point out in the Introduction, not all stress is undesirable. *Sometimes stress is good*. I offer the example of an athlete who is flat for a game. That person will probably not perform at top proficiency. Hence, Hall of Fame basketball Coach Bobby Knight was accustomed to putting pressure on his players, even during practice. He never allowed them to coast, once they had built a lead. He did not want them to be flat. When athletes are flat, their opponents often win. So, even with the three reasons you have offered yourself for calling your prospects, there may be a fear or two, a stress or two, which have not completely vanished. So be it. It simply means that you are not flat. It means that you **maintain enough stress to compete successfully**.

If I Don't Call My Prospects, I Will Make No Money

The final, and most economically important, reason for calling prospects involves syllogistic reasoning:

Major Premise: Salespersons must make sales appointments in order to generate income.

Minor Premise: If I call no prospects, no one will schedule an appointment.

Conclusion: If I call no prospects, I will have no income.

Salespersons may have difficulty seeing that **every single one** of the twenty-one sales **is necessary for producing income**, but, surely, **everyone can see the need for appointments**!

As a salesperson, there have been many days when I have not felt like making phone calls. It has nothing to do with fear. I just do not feel like working. Yet, on such days, I find available times on my appointment schedule that are blank.

I have **two options**--take an *unpaid vacation* from work or *make phone calls*. Don't get me wrong. I do believe that everyone needs a vacation now and then, but, in the sales profession, these vacations are usually unpaid. If I want to, I can give myself three days vacation each week, or even four, or five, or six, or seven. What a great boss I am for myself! Or, am I? **Employees love bosses who give vacations, but they hate bosses who cut their pay.** Whenever I skip phone calling, *I have a love-hate relationship with myself.*

I **always keep records** of my *phone contacts*, my *scheduled appointments*, my *kept appointments*, and my *money-exchanging sales*. I use **quantitative research: statistics.** I know *exactly how many kept appointments I need in order to make money.* I know *exactly how many scheduled appointments I need in order to have a kept appointment.* I know *how many phone contacts I need in order to have a scheduled appointment.* Bottom line: I know *how many phone contacts I need to make money.* **I can promise myself whatever income I want to.** I just **need to make the telephone calls.**

Caution: Of course, salespersons always need to **be aware of telemarketing laws** (both state and national) when calling prospects. In particular, **pay close attention to state and national "Do Not Call" laws.** Telemarketing laws, rules, and regulations are constantly changing, and violations can carry multi-thousand-dollar fines and legal fees. For information, the reader is directed to: **http://www.donotcallprotection.com/do_not_call_chart.shtml**, rather than listing detailed descriptions of laws state-by-state and nationally in this book. **You should not, however, use these laws as an excuse for not calling** prospects. **Typically**, as recommended in this book, **calling an individual for <u>research purposes</u>, rather than telephone sales purposes, is not a violation of these laws.** This book recommends a procedure of calling individuals **for research purposes**, and then, as a gesture of appreciation for the research information, offering to send the individuals a gift by mail. This **book does not advocate telephone <u>sales</u>**, per se.

TWENTY-ONE SALES: PART TWO

AUDIENCE = PHONE PROSPECT

SALE NUMBER SIX

You Should Give Me Just One Minute of Your Time

Subject: Giving me just one minute of your time.

Theme: Reasons for giving me just one minute of your time.

Proposition: You should give me just one minute of your time.

Interrogative: Why?

Key Word: Reasons.

Audience: Phone Prospect.

Objective: To persuade the phone prospect that s/he should give me just one minute of his/her time.

Divisions (i.e., "reasons"):

    1. I am courteous

    2. My name (and/or title) sounds legitimate

    3. My company (or business entity) sounds relevant to the prospect

    4. I promise not to take more than one minute

    Sale Number Six may be the **most difficult sale** to accomplish. This does not mean that it is the most stressful for either the salesperson or the phone prospect. Often, if it fails to succeed, neither the phone prospect nor the salesperson give it another thought. The attempt took only a few seconds. There has been no great investment in time on either person's part. No big deal, right? Perhaps it does not seem big because it is so small. Yet, it is a very important sale because it is **the very first interpersonal sale** that a salesperson must make.

This sale is *difficult because* it *must be made within a very few seconds*. There is **no time for an anecdote, case study, or scenario** but a certain type of ***pathos* must be generated**. The type of *pathos* or emotion that you want the phone prospect to experience might be called **interest** or **anticipation**. The type of ***pathos* that should be avoided** is **suspicion** or **boredom**. Whatever the emotion is called, clearly some emotion is needed. The absence of emotion is apathy. *Apathy is not what you want the phone prospect to experience*. How can you generate emotion without an anecdote, case study, or scenario?

This sale is *also difficult because* there is **no time for a developed logical argument**, yet a certain type of ***logos* must be generated**. Perhaps a quick **statistic** might work, but the phone prospect would need to be able to grasp the right **conclusion** within seconds: *I should give this person--a salesperson—just one minute of my time*. There is **usually no time for a full-blown syllogism (**but a **"rhetorical syllogism"**—otherwise known as an **"enthymeme"—will work**. If I were selling a water purification system to individuals in a certain area who are on well and septic systems, I might offer a **minor premise** (or a piece of **data**) to the phone prospect, "Did you know that *75 percent of the wells in your neighborhood have contaminated water?*" This is quick. I can only use this **statistic** if I have done needs research (**Sale Number One**) and market research (**Sale Number Four**), so that I know that this phone prospect probably has a need. However, if I have done the research, and my **data** is correct, a bright phone **prospect can supply most of the remaining elements of the syllogism (and even Toulminian analysis) by herself/himself** within a moment. This is how an **enthyme** works. The other elements that the phone prospect will automatically supply are:

> **Major Premise/Warrant**: (Since) People don't want their families to drink
> contaminated water,

> **Conclusion/Claim**: I should give this person one minute of my time.

Rebuttal 1: Unless I have already purchased a water purification system or otherwise handled the problem. (If this rebuttal is used, either I have failed to do enough market research *or this phone call may be considered the market research*, thus, saving valuable sales appointment time for those who have not taken care of the problem.)

Rebuttal 2: Unless this salesperson does not appear to have *ethos*. (**Backing**: *But*, how will the prospect know within the first few seconds whether I have *ethos*? This question will be dealt with shortly.)

Rebuttal 3: Unless this salesperson will ramble on for a long time, and I don't have time right now to listen. (The phone prospect must be reassured that this rebuttal does not apply.)

Rebuttal 4: Unless I don't even live in that neighborhood, or unless my home is on city water, or unless I have already had my water tested and it's okay. (These are rebuttals for which there is no good backing. They pertain to **relevance**. The phone prospect is saying, "Your phone call is not *relevant* to me." Some of these situations may be eliminated by doing more market research. Some of them may be considered market research. Some of them simply spell the end of the telephone conversation.)

Thinking through such a logical sequence, clearly four types of backing may be necessary. I will (here) refer to **these types of backing** as the **four reasons for the phone prospect to give me just one minute of his/her time**. However, **I do not state explicitly to the phone prospect** that *there are four reasons for giving me one minute of his/her time*. This sale is an extremely quick sale. It is an **implicit sale**. Much of the **logic is left unstated** but most **intelligent people will implicitly** and automatically **make the connections**.

This hypothetical phone call might begin:

"*Hello, Mrs. Bailey*?"

"Yes."

"Mrs. Bailey, this is Mr. Lindsay with the Aquanalysis Corporation, and we have new reports that show that the water in 75 percent of the wells in Richland subdivision have a high level of contamination. Would it be possible for me to have just one minute of your time today?"

I have offered only a piece of data, and have asked a question . . . or have I? Implicit in my question was also a **claim**: You should give me a minute of your time. As mentioned before, Mrs. Bailey is able to supply the **warrant**: Since I don't want my family to drink contaminated water. And, **I have implicitly offered four backings for her possible rebuttals**. They are the *four reasons she should give me a minute of her time.*

I am Courteous

When I *politely* **asked** if I was speaking to **Mrs. Bailey**, I showed courtesy. If I had said, "Let me speak to the woman of the house," I would have been discourteous. **Asking** is considered polite and courteous; demanding is not. Taking the time to **know someone's name** is courteous; calling her "the woman of the house" is not. Referring to someone who is an adult with a **title of respect (Mrs.)** is courteous; calling her by her first name (even if my market research has provided it) is not.

When I **introduced myself** to Mrs. Bailey, I showed courtesy. It would have been blunt and discourteous to have leaped immediately to my data, as follows:

"Hello, Mrs. Bailey?"

"Yes."

"We have new reports that show that the water in 75% of the wells in Richland subdivision have a high level of contamination."

She might wonder, "Who is this person, and who is the 'we' that has the reports?" Even if I were to identify myself as Stan Lindsay and to proceed to the data, she might still wonder, "So, who is Stan Lindsay and with whom is he connected?" The implication here is, "**What is this person trying to hide about himself and his company**?"

I know of some companies which recommend that their salespersons not identify the company during the entire phone call. Why? People would hang up. The companies have a reputation for wasting prospects' time. Once a company develops such a *reputation*, **Sale Number Six** becomes very difficult indeed! The problem is an *ethos* problem. People have grown to **distrust** the company. However, the solution to the problem is not to engender more distrust! **If someone does not** have the courtesy to **identify himself/herself** and the business entity which s/he represents, s/he **loses *ethos*** immediately.

When I asked Mrs. Bailey, "Would it be possible . . . ," I displayed courtesy. **Asking instead of demanding is not the entire issue here.** The point is that I did not ask her, "*Do you have a minute?*" Even if she has a minute, she *may not wish to spend it on the phone* with me. Furthermore, that she *may not have a minute right now* is *no indication that she has no interest* in what I am calling about. She may have something on the stove. She may be late for an appointment. She may have children who need to be tucked in. There are **many possible reasons that she does not have even one minute**, just now. By asking, "Would it be possible for me to have just one minute of your time today?" I have shown courtesy. She may answer, "Of course, but not right now." My response could then be: "Fine, when should I call back?"

Courtesy sends an implicit message of *ethos*. It partially *preempts the rebuttal*: Unless this salesperson *does not appear to have ethos*. It does *not completely* preempt that rebuttal, however. Along with the first reason (I am courteous), I would offer a *second reason*, which follows.

My Name (and/or Title) Sounds Legitimate

In the Aquanalysis example, I referred to **myself** as **Mr. Lindsay**. I could have said "Hi, this is Stan with Aquanalysis." Those who believe that sales are based upon establishing friendship *miss the boat here*. The issue is still an *ethos* issue. *Ethos* has two parts--expertise and active goodwill. Those who believe it is smarter to say "Hi, this is **Stan**" *probably believe* that this is a friendly greeting and, hence, establishes **goodwill**. On the contrary, many American cultural rules have been inherited from our European ancestors. Virtually **all European cultures** make distinctions between those instances in which we address another individual in **familiar** terms and those in which we address another individual in more **formal** terms. For example, as anyone who has studied German would know, it is offensive to use a familiar form of address when a formal form of address is appropriate. Hubert Jannach (1961) writes, "When speaking to children, relatives, or close friends, Germans use the **familiar** forms of address . . . . In all other situations, the **formal** . . . is used" (p. 4). Clearly, Mrs. Bailey is not a child, relative, or close friend of mine. I should not address her by her first name. By the same token, if I identify myself by my first name, **I have reduced my status, implicitly**. She knows that I am neither a relative nor a close friend, so what am I? A child?

Americans do **implicitly** what Germans do systematically. **Teachers** are called "**Mr. Lindsay**." **Students** are called "**Stan**." **Bosses** are called "**Mr. Lindsay**." **Employees** are called "**Stan**." **Presidents** are called "**President Lindsay**" (or so I wish). Ordinary **citizens** are called "**Stan**." I have had *salespersons* call me and *use my first name with impudence*. They even say, "Hey, buddy, this or that." *I tune them out*. They have *no right to assume familiarity* with me unless I agree to the status. By the same token, *if they offer me the right to assume familiarity with them, it immediately lowers their ethos implicitly*. I am allowed to view them as a "child" or "student" or "employee," etc. As a salesperson, it is prudent for me to **retain whatever *ethos* is derived by referring to myself as "Mr. Lindsay."** The "teacher, boss, and president" image is the image of one who has **expertise, hence, *ethos***. My courtesy in dealing with the prospect and **my use of the term Mrs. Bailey** help to provide a message of **active goodwill, the other element** of *ethos*.

Incidentally, **if you have the legitimate right to use a title** that implicitly carries *ethos*, you should, of course, use it. *Ethos* is earned. If you have earned the title, it is not immodest to use it. When I call someone on behalf of the College Benefit Program, I use the words, "This is **Dr.** Lindsay with the College Benefit Program." If I send material by mail, I use the letters "**Ph.D.**"

following my name. They supply *ethos*. My mention of the "College Benefit Program" brings us to the third reason that the phone prospect should give me a minute of his/her time.[5]

My Company (or Business Entity) Sounds Relevant to the Prospect

The **name of his/her business entity** or company should **implicitly suggest relevance**. I do not know if a water purification company named Aquanalysis exists. If it does, the name of the company sounds relevant to prospects who may have drinking water problems. By **adding the word "Corporation,"** I sometimes add *ethos*. Prospects will likely feel that a *corporation* may own the equipment to correctly analyze one's water, whereas, "Harry's Water Service" may or may not have the necessary equipment. For example, I was once contacted by a long distance landline telephone service which offered me substantially lower rates on all of my long distance phone calls. The name of the business entity was Pete's Telephone Service. I was not interested.

When I call phone prospects who are seniors and graduate students and state, "This is Dr. Lindsay with the **College Benefit Program**," an important part of **Sale Number Six** is made. My business entity sounds as if it may be relevant to the prospect.

I Promise Not to Take More Than One Minute

The fourth and final reason my prospect should give me one minute of his/her time is that I honestly promise not to take more than a minute. This reason provides **backing for Rebuttal 3**: *Unless this salesperson will ramble on for a long time, and I don't have time right now to listen.* By asking, **"Would it be possible to have just one minute of your time today?"** I have *preempted Rebuttal 3*. **How** did I accomplish this feat?

---

[5]The **first two reasons** that I have offered supply **backing for Rebuttal 2**: Unless this salesperson does not appear to have *ethos*. **Reason number three** supplies **backing for relevance-related *rebuttals***. Of course, if the problem has already been solved or if it really is irrelevant to this particular prospect, no backing will work. But, assuming that you have successfully completed the market research, reason number three should be offered.

First, my *courtesy* suggested that I could be trusted when I asked for one minute. **Second**, my **use of the term "just"** clearly communicated that I was *not using a figure of speech* when I said "minute of your time." **Third**, by using the term **"one" instead of "a,"** I have become quite specific. Consider the difference between *"a minute of your time"* and *"just one minute of your time."* If I use the *first phrasing*, it is easy for the phone prospect to come up with Rebuttal 3. If I use the *second phrasing*, it is **much more difficult**. Here, using Rebuttal 3 is much more tantamount to calling me a liar. Why would the phone prospect call me a liar after only five seconds? This is irrational.

The **objective** of this sale is only **to persuade the phone prospect to give me one minute of his/her time.** The use of a quick **statistic**, as in the Aquanalysis example, is only one approach to making the phone prospect believe that my phone call is relevant enough to allow me one minute. *It is not necessary to use statistics.* A **fact** might work. An example might be: "Mrs. Bailey, this is Mr. Lindsay with the Shoe Warehouse. I'm calling to let you know about a service that can save you 65 percent on the costs of name-brand athletic shoes for your children." An **authority** might work: "Mrs. Bailey, this is Mr. Lindsay with Smoke-Out. The *Surgeon General* claims that second-hand smoke is deadlier than first-hand smoke, but s/he certifies that methods such as those used by Smoke-Out provide an inexpensive method of purifying the air in your home. Would it be possible for me to have just one minute of your time today?"

Facts, **statistics**, and **authorities** may help **to establish enough relevance** in the first few seconds of a telephone call to persuade the phone prospect to give me one minute of his/her time. There is **not time for a full fledged scenario, case study, or anecdote**. However, **references to well-known stories** may **also** help to persuade the phone prospect to allow one minute. An example might be: "Mrs. Bailey, this is Mr. Lindsay with Masonry Contractors. We believe that the *third little pig* had the best idea, so we provide brick exteriors to existing homes. Would it be possible for me to have just one minute of your time today?"

Whether or not I use a **well-known story**, **fact**, **statistic**, or **authority**, by incorporating the four reasons that I have offered in **Sale Number Six**, the phone **prospect implicitly builds a scenario** of his/her own. It looks like this: *"A considerate, courteous, and respectable business person has called me on the phone to ask for only one minute of my time so that he might discuss something that sounds as if it could be* **relevant**[6] *to me. How can I not give him/her the one minute?"*

This sale has very close similarities to **Advertising**. In fact, this sale could be **made by** Advertising. In a **sixty-second television advertisement**, for example, the **commercial must sell** the viewer—**in the first few seconds**—that the viewer should **give the commercial message one minute of his/her time** to finish viewing the commercial. We call these first few seconds of a television commercial the **"attention"** step. If viewers are commonly willing to view the entire commercial, based on the attention step, we say that the advertisement has **"stickiness."** The first few seconds make the viewer *"stick around"* to watch the entire commercial. Otherwise, if the viewer is using **TiVo** or **DVR** to view the program, in what is called **time-shifting**, s/he may be inclined to **zip** through the commercial rather than watch it. If the viewer is not using TiVo or DVR to view the program, but is watching the program in real time, s/he may be inclined to **zap** the commercial (change channels) or to use the commercial break to use the restroom or to grab a snack or drink from the refrigerator. **Whenever the viewer zips or zaps**, this sale has not been made. The viewer has not granted the commercial "just one minute" of his/her time.

In **Radio Advertising**, the commercial may just fade out of attention and into background noise, if this sale is not made in the first few seconds. In **Print Advertising**, studies show that certain areas of the advertisement (**display copy**, such as **headlines**, photos, and captions) are

---

[6]Note that in **Sale Number Seven** I establish the proposition that the subject which I address is relevant enough for the phone prospect to become a prospect by being willing to consider more information on the subject. In **Sale Number Ten**, I begin to persuade the prospect to become a client by selling the prospect on the proposition that s/he has a problem/need. This is a further development of the relevance sale which begins in **Sale Number Six**. Each of these **relevance sales** accomplish a distinct objective at the time they are made. Just because a phone prospect is persuaded in a few seconds that the subject which I address sounds relevant enough to allow one minute of time does not mean that the phone prospect is persuaded that it is relevant enough to consider my proposal.

focused on first. If the readers interest is not is not engaged in the first few seconds, by the display copy, the **body copy** (full textual message) will not be read. **Emails** and other **Online Advertising methods** face even tougher tests. Often, there is only a **split-second opportunity** for an online ad to catch the reader's attention. In an email, the **subject line and sender** may be the only opportunity to capture attention. In **Outdoor Advertising** (such as billboards and messages on vehicles), the **split-second opportunity** extends frequently to the entire advertisement. If the viewer does not register the entire point of the billboard or vehicle message within just a few seconds, s/he is past the billboard and driving on! Therefore, the **objective** of the **first few seconds of any advertisement** is to secure the **attention/interest/stickiness** of the viewer/reader/driver (typically for up to one minute).

The methods for securing "just one minute" (or less) in other forms of marketing vary. In **Outdoor Advertising**, Chick Fil-A has successfully used **cutouts** of cows, writing "Eat Mor Chikin!" (with **child-like handwriting font** and **misspellings**) to gain attention. In **Print Advertising**, as mentioned above, **display copy** is often used to gain attention, but most successful attention steps in Print Advertising use **pictures**. In **Radio Advertising**, the **theater of the mind** may be used. **Sound effects** and **mood music** or the voice of (or a good impression of the voice of) a **famous person or character** can capture the listener's attention for the duration of a commercial. In **Television Advertising** (as in other Advertising), Burke's concept of **perspective by incongruity** is useful: a little girl talking with a grown man's deep voice, a gecko chatting in a British/Australian accent, etc. **Perspective by incongruity** occurs when two things do not seem to have **congruity**; *they do not logically seem to fit together*. This causes the viewer or listener to pause and pay attention to what is happening, to try to make sense of it.

The **objective** in Advertising attention steps, similar to the objective in **Sale Number Six**, is to get the viewer or listener or phone prospect to conclude: *How can I not give the commercial just one minute?"*

SALE NUMBER SEVEN

This Matter is Relevant to You

Subject: The relevance of this matter.

Theme: Reasons for the relevance of this matter.

Proposition: This matter is relevant to you.

Interrogative: Why?

Key Word: Reasons.

Audience: Phone Prospect.

Objective: To persuade the phone prospect that this matter is relevant to him/her.

Divisions (i.e., "reasons"):

　　1. You are the type of person for whom my business was created

　　2. You have needs to which this matter pertains

　　3. You probably are already interested in this matter

　　Sale Number Six has bought some time . . . but not much. You have asked for one minute of time from your telephone prospect and s/he has granted it. But you have already used ten seconds. In the **next fifty seconds**, you must sell the phone prospect that **this matter is relevant to him/her**, that **you are affiliated with a legitimate enterprise**, and that **it is worthwhile for him/her to consider more information on this subject.** Recall, however, that, in **Sale Number**

Six, *you have already begun* making all three of these sales. Specifically, with regard to **relevance**, you have already mentioned *the name of your business entity*. This name should immediately sound relevant to your phone prospect. In fact, the phone prospect may already implicitly have a host of expectations regarding your phone call based simply on the name of my business entity. Perhaps your business entity has done a great deal of **advertising** and the phone prospect **has** been **exposed to the types of services that your business entity provides**. Your job now involves making certain that your phone prospect clearly sees the relevance of your services to him/her. Envision essentially **three reasons for the relevance of your services** to the phone prospect:

- S/he is the **type of person for whom your business was created.**
- S/he has **needs to which this matter pertains**.
- S/he is probably **already interested in this matter**.

You Are the Type of Person for Whom My Business Was Created

The **first step** in establishing relevance is **classification**. You want to **place your phone prospect quickly in the class of individuals whom your business serves**. If a salesperson calls me to explain that s/he has a wonderful offer for sport fishermen, I get off the phone immediately. I am not in the class of sport fishermen. If someone calls to say s/he offers estate planning, I excuse myself. I do this type of thing, myself. I am not in the class of those who need the service marketed to them. If someone calls to discuss female products, I halt the discussion. I am not a female. The salesperson has not paid attention to class.

When **I call college seniors and graduate students**, after securing one minute of their time, I continue, "*We're sending a free recorded financial benefits message to the **seniors and graduate students who will be finishing up within the next twelve months**, and I understand that you will be finishing in May of* [*such and such year*]; *is that correct?*" Obviously, I cannot project a graduation date if I have not completed some **market research**. I could be wasting enormous amounts of time, if I do not have *a fairly reliable list of students who are close to graduating*. Implicitly, the **phone prospect recognizes this fact**. This phone call is not one of those random "call everybody who has a phone number" solicitations. The prospect begins to think, "This matter must be somewhat relevant to me."

You Have Needs to Which This Matter Pertains

Once you have *classified* the phone prospect, **clarify** somewhat the reason(s) for serving this specific classification. What **needs**, **goals**, **problems**, or **concerns** are special *for this classification*? Within the few seconds that are available, it will be impossible to specify the exact needs, goals, problems, and concerns of the phone prospect. The sale must be made **implicitly**. Implicit in the list that I provide at this point are the specific applications that the phone prospect might make to his/her individual situation.

After I have classified my phone prospect for the College Benefit Program (and corroborated or corrected my earlier market research), I proceed with a **list of needs** that my business entity addresses:

> *The recorded financial benefits message takes only about 17 minutes to listen to, but it provides information on how to **save $1000 per year on new car payments**, how to **earn the equivalent of almost 7 percent guaranteed interest** on your savings (as compared to a "taxable" investment such as a bank CD), a **better retirement program than an IRA**, various **insurance benefits**, and free financial planning advice.*

I know that many of my phone prospects will be **buying a new car** within the next year or two. Most of them will have extra money soon for **savings and investment** purposes. Virtually all of them will be looking at **benefits packages** with the companies that hire them. They can use some **advice** in all of the areas of financial planning. I rapidly hint at needs that my phone prospect might face in the near future. I have not answered any of these needs, yet. **My goal**

here is only to establish relevance. If my business entity and the resulting classification of phone prospects were different, my list of suggested needs would be different. You must determine the needs that phone prospects in the classification to whom you are marketing experience. You must make certain that the list of needs that are addressed is relevant.

You Probably Are Already Interested in This Matter

I would guess that **most college seniors and graduates have given some thought** to some of the issues/needs that I mention. If they have not given these matters thought, it is getting close to the point **they will need to**. I might explicitly state, "You probably have already begun to consider some of these matters." Or, I might simply assume that they have. The list should include at least one or two issues that already interest the phone prospect. If this is not the case, it may be difficult to make this sale.

I personally must be on some **inaccurate market research** list designed to identify homeowners who might need replacement windows. My home is five years old. It really does not need replacement windows. Yet, at least once every other week, it seems, someone will call me to tell me about a special offer on windows for my home. Those who call have not sufficiently researched the market. Frankly, I am beginning to tire of these calls. I am reluctant to give the salesperson even one minute of my time, anymore. The matter is simply **not relevant** to me.

If I were selling replacement windows, **I would do the market research** to identify those neighborhoods with older homes. I would **consider broadening my services/products** to include solar room additions, screened-in porches, gazebos, remodeling projects, and storage sheds. I would **use a telephone market research approach** before I would consider anyone whom I have called a phone prospect. The market research phone conversation can be very short: "Mrs. Bailey, this is Mr. Lindsay. I'm conducting market research for Remodeling,

Incorporated. Would it be possible for me to have just one minute of your time, today?" If she grants me the minute, I would ask, "If you were able to afford a remodeling project on your home right now, what would you do first?" This is what is called a **direct open-ended question**[7] (a question that *gives you some control over the interview but does not limit the response*). If she could not think of anything right away, I might shift the question to a **closed-ended question** (one in which I *offer a list of answers from which she might choose*): "Let me suggest a few possible projects. If one of these applies, just say "yes": solar room addition, screened-in porch, gazebo, windows, doors, kitchen, bath, storage shed?" If she has identified any product or service which my business entity handles, I would say, "Thank you very much, Mrs. Bailey. As a token of my appreciation for your help, I'd like to send you a free gift. You'll receive it by mail in a day or two." I would verify her mailing address. Then, I would get off the phone.

If I do not get off the phone, I am a liar. I identified my call as **market research**. If I turn it into a **sales call**, I have lost *ethos*. There will be plenty of time to phone Mrs. Bailey after I have mailed her the free gift that I promised. The **free gift should relate to the product or service that I offer** which she has indicated is potentially **relevant** to her. Depending on whether or not her relevant interest is a big ticket item for me, I will mail her a more expensive or less expensive gift. **Later**, when I make a follow up call to her, **she will trust me to keep my word** about the length of time I intend to keep her on the phone. She will also be more inclined to find out about my product/service because it will be **relevant** to her.

Relevance, when considered from a **consumer behavior** approach, is sold by using **vivid stimuli**. What is vivid to one person may not be vivid to another. This means that *vivid stimuli* capture the **attention of some of the people all of the time**; whereas, **salient stimuli** capture the **attention of all of the people some of the time**. There is an interesting example of **External Transit Advertising** (one variety of **Out Of Home** Advertising) in which a local zoo has painted a city bus to appear that it is being **constricted by a huge python** that has coiled around the bus

---

[7]Courtland L. Bovee and John V. Thill (1995), *Business communication today* (4th ed.). New York: McGraw-Hill, 577.

several times and is squeezing the life out of the bus. This advertisement certainly catches the attention. We may say it uses **salient stimuli** because it *stands out in a crowd*. **Everyone** notices it. But for us to say that it uses **vivid stimuli**, we need to recognize that not everyone is interested in zoos. **Some people**, however, love zoos. Therefore, an advertisement about a local zoo is **relevant** to those people. The External Transit Advertising would be supplying *vivid stimuli* to those to whom zoos are *relevant*. In the area of sales, we are *far more concerned* in **Sale Number Seven** with *vivid stimuli* than with *salient stimuli*. We have a **target market**. We are not trying to sell the entire public. We only want to capture the **attention of some of the people, not all of the people**.

SALE NUMBER EIGHT

I am a Legitimate Enterprise

Subject: My legitimacy.

Theme: Indicators of my legitimacy.

Proposition: There are three indicators of my legitimacy.

Interrogative: What?

Key Word: Indicators.

Audience: Phone Prospect.

Objective: To persuade the phone prospect that I am a legitimate enterprise.

Divisions (i.e., "indicators"):

1. My prior reputation
2. My business entity's prior reputation
3. Your first impression of me

As was the case with the sale of relevance (**Sale Number Seven**), *this sale has already begun* in **Sale Number Six**. Already, my *ethos* and the *ethos* of my business entity have been somewhat presented.

The fact that I have been *courteous* has encouraged the phone prospect to categorize me among those business persons with whom s/he is willing to do business. I have *asked* for, not demanded, information. I have *introduced my business entity and myself* immediately. I have not hidden this information. Since my phone call was unsolicited, I have requested *only one minute* of the phone prospect's time. This is not too presumptuous.

I have also *used terminology that presents my business entity and me as legitimate.* I have introduced myself as Mr. Lindsay or Dr. Lindsay instead of Stan. I may have used the term corporation when introducing my business entity. This terminology implies legitimacy. (Note, however, that *legally a salesperson cannot claim that his/her company is a corporation if it is not.* I must only claim credentials that are valid.) Now, however, I have a few seconds in which to expand on my *ethos* and the *ethos* of my company.

Public communication specialists Neher, Waite, Cripe, and Flood (1994) identify the concept of **initial *ethos***: "the audience's impression of the speaker before the speech is delivered . . . [it] has two elements: **prior reputation** and **first impressions**" (p. 252). Initial *ethos* is precisely what I am attempting to sell in **Sale Number Eight** Thus, in making the sale that I am a legitimate enterprise, I would offer three indicators of my legitimacy: **my prior reputation**, **my business entity's prior reputation**, and the phone prospect's **first impression of me.**

My Prior Reputation

One term that dictionaries use to help define the term "**repute**" is "**account.**" I find this term to be more panoramic than "honor" or "credit" or "fame." The term "account" conjures up a **mathematical entelechy** in which both credits and debits are measured against each other to produce a current balance. Unavoidably, in a sales career, there will be some phone prospects, some sales prospects, and (possibly) some clients who **harbor negative attitudes** toward me. Every great person in history has had those who considered themselves his/her opponents. Yet, there are also those who have **found my assistance to be quite beneficial**, who have found me quite likable, and who, in accordance with **Sale Number Twenty-One**, would provide a reference for me. In other words, my **reputation** includes **both positives and negatives.**

Every contact that I make in my career or in my personal life can be found somewhere in the accounting book that is my reputation. If my livelihood depends upon my reputation (and, in sales, it does to a great degree), I should seriously consider my actions toward people. When Moses provided the Ten Commandments to Israel, he provided rules not only for getting along with God, but also **rules for getting along with other people**. If I fail to honor my parents, it goes in my reputation accounting book. If I literally murder or even figuratively commit character assassination, it goes in the book. If am unfaithful to my spouse, it is accounted against me. If I steal or otherwise cheat people, my reputation book records it. Similarly, if I lie about my product, give fake statistics, or claim an endorsement that does not exist (or, as mentioned earlier, ask for only one minute when I plan to take five), this becomes a part of my reputation.

There are **no simple remedies for a bad reputation**, but there are **some things** that can be done to **present our reputations more positively**. I cannot write a chapter in this book that will help to erase everything that has been written in the book of reputation that every person writes. In many ways, we must simply live with the reputations we develop. My reputation (and the reputation of every other salesperson) speaks for itself. Nevertheless, no one can be expected to have an absolutely 100 percent positive reputation accounting balance. So, **how do I go about establishing initial *ethos* if there are some who would supply negatives**?

First, I should identify for myself **those who are likely to provide a positive reference** for me. **Second**, I should **categorize** them. **Third**, I should **link my categories to the specific phone prospect** to whom I am speaking. Most of us do this haphazardly, anyway. I simply suggest that we do this systematically.

The **best source** of individuals who are likely to provide a positive reference for me is my **client base**. This is why **Sale Number Twenty-One** is so important! Once I gain a client who is willing to provide a reference for me, I **consider the categories of phone prospect** into which this person fits. If the client has offered me *specific referrals*, I know that I have reputation working for me when I contact the individuals recommended. In my market, I also categorize my clients (on paper) according to *fraternity or sorority membership*, *major* field of study, *street* *address* or *dormitory address*, etc. I do not throw away this information, even after an individual has graduated and moved away. Sometimes, a senior will know or will have heard about a person (from his fraternity or her major) who graduated years before. I will **insert this suggested reference nonchalantly** into the phone conversation, thus: "Perhaps, you know one of my clients from your sorority . . . ." Then, I will list a few, beginning with the most recent. Even if the phone prospect never mentions my name to the reference, or *vice versa*, there is an element of legitimacy that results from my possessing such a reference.

My Business Entity's Prior Reputation

The same factors that apply to your reputation also apply to the reputation of your business entity. No matter how great a reputation you may possess, if your business entity owns a poor reputation, you may have difficulty making **Sale Number Eight**. Companies are sometimes impervious toward this fact. They believe that it is your job to make the sale, not theirs. I know, of course, that some responsibility rests with each entity--the company and the salesperson.

Every other salesperson who has ever sold for the business entity for which you are selling **has affected the reputation** of your business entity. This is scary, but true. You may be a very ethical member of an organization, but if the person to whom you have introduced yourself knows you only as a member of the organization and knows one or more scoundrels from the organization, you have lost some initial *ethos*.

If there is **a quick fact or statistic or quote from an authority** that will establish the legitimacy of your business entity, you should use it. If your **business entity supports charitable organizations** with which the phone prospect identifies, you should mention the fact (or, the phone prospect may already know the fact). If your business entity does a good deal of **advertising**, your phone prospect may have picked up some legitimizing influence there.

One specific type of Advertising—**Specialty Advertising**--places the brand's name on a product such as a T-shirt, which it then gives away. An example of Specialty Advertising that I thought was particularly useful in my market was used when the company supplied those foam rubber hands with the index finger extended to make the sports-associated message "We're Number One!" They were provided in the school colors, and on the back of the hand was printed the company name and logo. Students could identify with the symbolism of the hand and, by extension, they could identify with the company that supplied it. (**My company was also #1** in the College Market!)

If your business entity is **relatively unknown, but is connected to another entity that has a strong positive reputation**, use it. I once represented a company of which none of my prospects had heard. Yet, this company was a *member of the Sears Financial Network*. When I introduced the company, I added the words, "a member of the Sears Financial Network." This added legitimacy to my company.

If your business entity is unknown, is not connected to any known business entity, and there are no quick facts, etc., which will establish legitimacy, you must face the fact that **you gain no initial *ethos*** from your business entity's prior reputation. On the other hand, since reputation is an accounting book, **you do not lose any initial *ethos*** from the entity's prior reputation, either. You simply must rely on your personal reputation and/or the phone prospect's first impression of you.

Your First Impression of Me

Besides **being courteous**, what else can you do to make a good first impression? If you were meeting someone **in person**, you could *dress professionally* and *be well-groomed*, but this encounter is **over the phone**. There is *no visual impression*. The **only option** available to you in the **nonverbal communication** area pertains to what is variously called **vocalics** or **paralanguage** or **paralinguistics**.

Interpersonal communication specialists Trenholm and Jensen (1992) identify **three basic components of the vocal system**--vocal *qualities*, vocal *characterizers*, and vocal *segregates*. Of these three components, the **one component to be avoided** in the telephone discussion is

vocal segregates. These are "*sounds that get in the way of fluent speech*, including 'uhs' and 'ums,' stuttering, and uncomfortable silences" (p. 196). **The more vocal segregates used, the less *ethos* is presented to the phone prospect.** If, uh, you, uh, were, um, . . . (long silence) to c-c-c-conv-v-converse in this, uh, fashion, uh, you, uh, would . . . (long silence) uh, probably, uh, lose, um, *ethos*. The person to whom you are speaking on the phone would **consider you to be lacking confidence and/or competence**. Hence, if you have a problem with vocal segregates, you need to **write out what you will be saying** and repeatedly **practice** what you have written.

"**Vocal qualities** include such things as *loudness, pitch, inflection, tempo, rhythm, intensity, articulation,* and *resonance*." (p. 196). Since the overall impression that you are trying to communicate is legitimacy, **excessive volume is counterproductive**. If someone shouts at me on the phone, I consider the behavior to be pushy. On the other hand, **if someone speaks too softly**, I think of the speaker as reticent or secretive, not fully confident. Volume should be loud enough to be easily understood (period).

Pitch is a *musical term*. Sopranos and tenors are able to produce a *high pitch*; basses produce a *low pitch*. If you speak in an extremely low pitch, as does Darth Vader, you appear to be **somewhat bored** with your business entity. If you speak in an extremely high pitch, like Mickey Mouse, you sound **too hyper**. Performance studies specialist R. E. Smith (1994) comments: "No ideal pitch exists except *in terms of each individual's range*. The **best pitch** for a person is called the *optimum pitch* and is located **one-fourth to one-third from the *bottom* of the pitch range**. At this point, a person can speak most comfortably and efficiently" (p. 284).

Inflection is the *pattern of rising or lowering pitch* in the course of speaking. *Rising inflection* seems to occur automatically *when you ask a question*. *Lowering inflection* occurs *when you make a statement*. Notice the inflection when you say, "Hello, Mrs. Bailey?" Did your pitch rise at the end? Now, say "This is Dr. Lindsay." Did your pitch lower at the end? Now say the same two phrases, but exchange the two inflections. Did "Hello, Mrs. Bailey?" sound like a statement? Did "This is Dr. Lindsay," sound like a question? There are times when it is courteous to phrase your message as a question. Yet, you must **be careful not to use the (questioning) rising inflection when making assertions**, your statements of fact. Your vocalics must reinforce the legitimacy of the fact. You must not say "The well water in your neighborhood is contaminated?" with a rising inflection. It sounds as if you do not know whether this fact is true or not. You need to legitimize your fact with a lowering inflection.

Resonance is essentially a full voice quality--the vibrancy which you might expect to hear from a radio announcer. The reason radio announcers are hired to read the text of commercials is that their voices are trained to be **comforting-yet-commanding**. You must be careful, however, to **avoid the exaggerated** "theatrical" or "sports announcer" voice styles. The phone call should be conducted in the relaxed, **conversational style** of a morning, drive-time, talk show host.

The **tempo**, or the *speed at which you speak*, should be *moderate*--not too fast (like a slick salesman), not too slow (like a dunce). The **intensity**, I believe, should be *low*. You should send no message, verbal or nonverbal, that sounds high-pressured. **Articulation** should be *clear*, but *not exaggerated*. Whenever you exaggerate your articulation, it causes your message to sound canned and it appears to send a *condescending* message, as if the person on the other end of the line may be a child who needs to have each word clearly pronounced.

Let's turn now to Trenholm and Jensen's (1992) third component: "**Vocal characterizers are more specific sounds that we may occasionally recognize as speech acts themselves**. *Laughing, crying, moaning, yelling*, and *whining* are examples" (p. 196). As the name suggests, vocal characterizers **indicate the character of the speaker**. Think of motion picture characters. What kind of non-verbal messages are sent by the vocalics of Harrison Ford as Indiana Jones, James Earl Jones as Darth Vader, Sylvester Stallone as Rocky? Vocal characterizers that salespersons use (often without realizing it) are:

- **The defeated character**--as if you have not made a sale in the past three weeks and you doubt that you will ever make another sale in your life;

- **The bored character**--as if you have been on the phone forever and you can't stop yawning while talking to your phone prospect;

119

- **The mother**--when you speak to your phone prospect so sweetly and nicely that you are condescending, thus, "Now, Mrs. Bailey, be a good girl and give me one minute of your time," and;

- **The sports announcer**--as if you are Dick Vitale saying "Hey, baby, the Aquanalysis Corporation is super, baby!"

These vocal characterizers **should be avoided**. You should *not even be so happy* in your phone conversation that you laugh throughout it, but something less than laughing is good. I learned early in my sales career that it was useful to sit in front of a mirror while talking on the phone. I try to **notice my facial expression**. If my face looks *bored*, my voice probably sounds bored. If I look *defeated*, my voice probably sounds defeated. If I *force myself to smile*, my vocalics will often follow suit. This is the desirable vocal characterizer. You must be **pleased** to have the opportunity to speak to the phone prospect, but you should *not be too giggly*. This is a pleasant business conversation.

I do **not** believe it is **wise** *to sell your company or yourself much further* to the phone prospect. The sale should be *mostly implicit*. If you begin to list your credentials at this point, you sound as if you have called to **brag**. This is not legitimacy.

Relevance (from **Sale Number Seven**) and **Credibility/Legitimacy** (from **Sale Number Eight**) are **absolutely essential matters** to address in the first few seconds of any message that you actually want people to listen to or read. **Relevance** answers the question: "Why should I care about *this subject*?" **Credibility** answers the question: "Why should I listen to *you* on this issue? If your audience believes that the issue you raise on the phone is relevant to him/her and that you are a credible/legitimate source of information for learning more about the issue, why would they not want to hear more?

SALE NUMBER NINE

It is Worthwhile for You to Consider More Information on This Subject

Subject: Considering more information on this subject.

Theme: Reasons for considering more information on this subject.

Proposition: You should consider more information on this subject.

Interrogative: Why?

Key Word: Reasons.

Audience: Phone Prospect.

Objective: To persuade the phone prospect to consider more information on this subject.

Divisions (i.e., "reasons"):

1. This matter is relevant to you

2. I am a legitimate enterprise

3. You will be able to conveniently consider the additional information

This is the final sale of **Part Two**. If this sale is not made, the sales process stops here. You are **not yet attempting to produce an exchange of money**. Your **objective** is only *to persuade the phone prospect to consider more information on the subject that you have presented*. You have used up the minute that the phone prospect has granted you. You *must not go further* without permission. Yet, *further information should appear useful* to the phone prospect. **Sale**

Number Seven and **Sale Number Eight** have provided the first two reasons the sales prospect should consider more information. The **reason that remains** to be provided is that the phone prospect will be able to *conveniently* consider the additional information.

Before you ask the phone prospect to accept delivery of further information, as a salesperson, you must **determine the most expedient and convenient method** for providing the additional information. **Several optional methods** exist--*telephone, printed material, audio recording, video recording, web page, podcast, seminar session,* and *sales interview*. Let's consider some **advantages and disadvantages** of each.

Telephone

On rare occasions, the phone prospect will ask you for the additional information *right then*, on the telephone. This prospect considers the telephone to be the most convenient method of receiving the information. S/he has **no chrono-stress, at this time**. S/he is willing to listen to a presentation of further information over the phone. **Advantages for the prospect** may be:

- Since s/he has the time right now to listen, this is the most convenient method.
- S/he may feel more protected from a (possibly pushy) salesperson speaking by phone rather than in person.
- If s/he has a question, s/he may ask it immediately.
- S/he may believe that there is no way that a monetary exchange may be made by phone.

Of course, this belief is erroneous. **Credit card** telephone sales are commonplace.

Disadvantages for the prospect may be:

- Most people seem to resent lengthy telemarketing conversations.
- In most situations, since the phone call was spontaneous, time has not been allotted for receiving detailed information over the phone.

- The prospect has **only one *sensory* channel** available for receiving the information in this situation: hearing. Some information may be more clearly presented by using sight, taste, touch, and/or smell.

Not only should the delivery system be convenient and expedient *for the prospect*, it should also be convenient and expedient *for you*. **Advantages for the salesperson** who uses a telephone delivery system for sharing additional information are:

- You may answer any questions that arise, immediately.
- There are financial savings: postage, gasoline, secretarial expense, printing expenses, etc.
- If the phone prospect is already clearly interested, there is no elapsed time that might cause the individual to lose interest.
- If the additional information is brief, you can manage time better by supplying the information now.

You should do this by phone, however, **only** if the prospect specifically offers to receive the information by phone. Otherwise, you have not kept your word about the one minute, and will lose *ethos*.

　Disadvantages for the salesperson who uses a telephone delivery system may be:

- Delivering further information at this time cuts into phone prospecting time. You will not be able to call as many prospects.
- You could easily and inexpensively use the services of a telephone secretary to make the initial contact. If the phone prospect wishes more information at the time of the phone call, it might require your personal service.
- You might be able to make a better presentation (and, hence, experience better results) using a different method of delivery.
- You may need to be quite careful that this phone call is categorized as market research, and not as telephone sales, due to **telemarketing laws**.

Printed Material

Using printed material as a delivery method has the following **advantages for the prospect**:

- The prospect does not need to spend time on the phone right now.

- The material will be conveniently delivered to his/her mailbox.

- By using the U. S. Postal service, if the business entity lies, it will be committing **mail fraud**. A legitimate business entity should have no qualms about allowing prospects to evaluate printed materials sent by mail. You or your telephone secretary should emphasize the legitimizing aspects of the fact that the prospect will be receiving printed materials by mail. It is advantageous not only to know that the business entity would not risk committing mail fraud, but also to further evaluate the legitimacy of the business in detail.

- The prospect will be able to consider the information at his/her convenience.

- If s/he loses interest, there is no need to look at the information.

- Printed material will allow the prospect to see any visuals, graphs, etc., which might enhance his/her understanding of the subject.

- S/he has already heard some information. Perhaps, smell and/or touch may also be communicated by this method.

Disadvantages for the prospect may be:

- The prospect will not be able to ask questions while working through the material.

- His/her most convenient available time might be the time spent driving to work, during which time, s/he cannot be "looking" at or "reading" printed materials.

- Printed materials seem impersonal.

- The prospect may not have the time to read through lengthy printed material. It may seem like a hassle.

Advantages for the salesperson might be:

- Printed materials easy to distribute--just put the information in an envelope and mail it.

- Printed materials often inexpensive to provide. Frequently, the salesperson's company will provide all of the printed materials needed, free of charge. Postage is affordable.

- Other than a computer-generated cover letter, the material does not need to be personalized.

- Printed materials often present a very professional image.

    Disadvantages for the salesperson might be:

- The prospect might not read the material.

- The prospect might have unanswered questions.

- You have worked to get the prospect; and should not entrust the possible sale to sales literature. If it were possible to make sales solely by mailing printed material, there would be no need for a salesperson.

Audio Recordings

In my agency, I finally settled on audio recordings as **my preferred method of delivery** for the next amount of information in the sales process. An audio recording combines many of the *advantages of telephone delivery* with many of the *advantages of printed material*. The advantages for the prospect are:

- The prospect may have time to listen while driving to work or elsewhere; this may be the most convenient method.

- The prospect may feel more protected from a (possibly pushy) salesperson by listening to a recording of that individual rather than in person.

- The prospect knows that there is no way that a monetary exchange may be made while s/he is listening to a recording.

- The prospect does not need to spend time on the phone.

- The material will be delivered to the prospect's mailbox.

- By using the U. S. Postal service, there is less possibility that the salesperson would make fraudulent claims due to the laws against mail fraud.

- The prospect will be able to consider the information at his/her convenience.

- If the prospect loses interest, there is no need to listen to the information further.

- Printed material may be included in the mailing, which will allow the prospect to see any visuals, graphs, etc., that might enhance his/her understanding of the subject. Perhaps, smell and/or touch may also be communicated by this method.

There are only two obvious **disadvantages for the prospect**:

- S/he will not be able to ask questions as s/he works through the material.

- S/he may not have access to a playback device.

The second possible disadvantage is rather remote. Most people have audio players (CD, jump drive, ipod, smart phone audio capability, etc.) in their home and auto, as well as on their person. It is wise to ask the prospect what medium of audio recording s/he prefers to receive.

What about **advantages for the salesperson**? They are:

- There are financial savings on gasoline and office space. You do not need to travel to the prospect's home or to provide office space for this presentation.

- If the additional information is lengthy, you can manage time better by supplying the information on audio recording.

- Recording media are reasonably inexpensive to provide. The postage required is relatively inexpensive.

- Along with a computer-generated cover letter, it is easy to personalize the audio recording. In my business, I simply put a personal tag line like "Hi, Mr. Jones" at the first of the recording, and the prospect feels that the entire recording was produced freshly for her/him.

- An audio recording is fairly easy to distribute. After personalizing and copying the material on the recording, you just put the material in an envelope and mail it.

- Along with any additional printed material that you may enclose, an audio recording presents both a very professional and a very personal image.

- The prospect is more likely to listen to the recording than to read printed material.

- Although some businesses are sending out audio recordings, it is still a unique and much more individualized approach than sending printed matter.

- An audio recording gives the prospect the notion that s/he has received an object (equivalent to a gift) from you. This builds *ethos* in the area of active goodwill.

- You also create *ethos* by making information available in a totally non-pressure context. The prospect cannot easily accuse you of pushing for a quick sale immediately.

- You can create even more *ethos* by pointing out that the prospect received the audio recording by mail. A business which intentionally provided false information through the mail would be guilty of mail fraud.

- An audio recording helps to satisfy a feeling in the prospect that s/he needs to get to know you somewhat before purchasing something from you. If the prospect has spoken to you by phone, and, now, hears your voice on the audio recording, when you finally meet in person, it will be the third contact. This will not be a hasty decision on the prospect's part.

The **disadvantages for the salesperson** are:

- The prospect might not listen to the recording.

- The prospect might have unanswered questions, after listening to the presentation.

Clearly, I believe, for my market, audio recordings are an excellent method of information delivery.

<u>Video Recordings</u>

Video recordings have **many of the same advantages and disadvantages as audio recordings**. The **disadvantage for the prospect** lies, primarily, in the *convenience of viewing the recording*. The prospect can listen to an audio recording while driving. A video recording requires time out of the prospect's home life. Family members may be watching TV at the times the prospect wishes to view the video recording. The **disadvantages for the salesperson** lie, primarily, in the fact that the video recording is *more expensive to purchase and produce, more time-consuming to dub*, and much *more inconvenient to personalize*.

On the positive side **(an advantage for the salesperson)**, a video that is professionally produced can be quite persuasive. Television has proven to be a very effective advertising medium. By sending information on video recording, you are essentially paying for TV Advertising on a *selective person-by-person basis*. Rather than waste money running advertisements to non-prospects, sending video recordings only to those who have expressed a willingness to receive further information is **extremely precise target marketing for TV commercials**.

It is **not necessary to mail** out videos, either. For several years, I invited prospects to come to my office for appointments. Rather than provide all of the information in person, which I found exhausting, I prepared a 25 minute video for prospects to watch before talking to me. By the time they were ready to talk to me, some of the sales in **Part Three** had already been accomplished.

Internet and Mobile Technologies

The computer age arrived decades ago. Certainly, computer technology is advancing so rapidly, there is a **temptation to use every new** app and feature in every market. The new technology, however, should be **used efficiently**. **Disadvantage for salespersons**: Not all new features and apps are used by enough individuals in every target market to make their use **efficient**. I have already mentioned the use of *jump drives*, *ipods*, and *smart phone* audio capability as options for conveying audio recordings. Salespersons are tempted, however, to employ new **innovations** before they have been sufficiently **diffused** to the general population. Those who study the **Diffusion of Innovations** list four types of consumers:

- **innovators** (those who are among the first to try new technologies and products),
- **early adopters** (those who are willing to try the innovations after innovators have tested them),
- **early majority** (the first major influx of many new users)

- **late majority** (the second major influx of many new users)

- **laggards** (those who are the last to try new technologies and products)

As you can see by the following chart curve, *innovators* and *early adopters* represent a total of only 16% of the population. *Early* and *late majority* users, on the other hand, represent 68% of the population. When *combined* with the *innovators and early adopters, the early and late majority* users represent a total of 84% of the population.

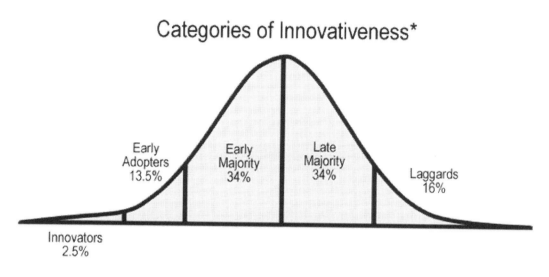

Categories of Innovativeness*

*From E.M. Rogers, *Diffusion of Innovations*, 4th edition (New York: The Free Press, 1995)

Advantages for salespersons and prospects: If salespersons prudently gauge the innovativeness of their target market to determine whether it is efficient to utilize a newly-developed technology as a means of disseminating information, the use of the new technology not only adds *convenience* **for both salespersons and prospects**, but also *ethos* **for salespersons,** as the prospect develops more respect for the salesperson due to his/her ability to use the latest technology.

Old standbys—*E-mail, texting,* and *social media*—provide the **fastest** and usually **least expensive** transmission of messages (an **advantage for salespersons and prospects**). Putting phones and computers together produced voicemail. Another **advantage for the salesperson** is that both the written messages of E-mail and the audible messages of voicemail can be **sent to**

any number of mailboxes, simultaneously. (Of course, technology also allows for audible messages to be **transposed** to written messages, and *vice versa*.) The messages can be **deleted, saved, and/or forwarded** to other mailboxes.

Disadvantage for salespersons: E-mail accounts may fill up quickly with **spam**. It is easier to expunge spam from an E-mail account or from voice mail than it is to dispose of hard copy junk mail. It is quite possible that **spam filters** will cause prospects to lose track of correspondence, as well.

Websites have **advantages for salespersons.** They are often *high-impact, state-of-the-art* cyberspace locations where individuals interested in knowing more about a particular company, person, or organization can browse. *Pictures, text,* and *graphics,* as well as *audio* and *video messages* may be stored at the website for prospects to consider. *Music* may be added to the message at the website using **MIDI** (Musical Instrument Digital Interface) capabilities. Multimedia effects (available in software packages) can add a professional appearance to the presentation. **Search engine optimization** [SEO] can develop preferred outcomes among the various search engines, so that the salesperson's message may be **received by other prospects**, beyond those whom the salesperson and his/her telephone secretaries have contacted. **Blogs**, either on the salesperson's website or on major sites such as blogger.com can increase traffic to the salesperson's website, or suggest other products the consumer may be interested in.

Well-produced **computer-generated presentations** may be used in countless ways. Computer-generated presentations may be used in **seminar selling**. The message that has been produced on the computer may be transferred to a large screen television or to a computer projection screen. **Teleconferencing**, "which encompasses **audioconferencing** and **videoconferencing** via phone lines and satellites"[8] has become increasingly common.

Disadvantage for salespersons: It is heartening to know that **people still prefer communicating with people** rather than computers. According to a recent survey, 95 percent of

---

[8]Bovee and Thill (1995), 97.

those questioned preferred reaching a person rather than a computer on their first call to a business.[9] New computer technologies are developing every day. The wise salesperson will continually consider how these technologies may be profitably used.

Seminars

Other than a personal interview, a **seminar** is the method that has the **advantage for both salespersons and prospects** of providing for the *closest personal contact between the salesperson and the prospect*. Some salespersons have used the method quite successfully. A seminar does not necessarily provide the information in a more personalized way than a video recording does, but it gives you an opportunity to answer questions immediately and to follow-up on interested prospects immediately.

Advantage (or disadvantage) for salespersons: There is something of a **herd mentality** among human beings. If a number of individuals at the seminar respond **favorably** to the sales message, some prospects will follow the herd. **However**, if **several leave** the seminar unconvinced, the herd mentality may work against you. My personal preference has always been to deal with prospects one at a time. I would rather let my message stand or fall by itself.

Recall that the objective in **Sale Number Nine** is to persuade the phone prospect to consider more information on the subject. **Convenience** has been a major selling point--the prospect must be able to *conveniently* consider the additional information. **Disadvantage for the prospect**: It is possible that the time or the length or the location of the seminar will be inconvenient for the prospect.

Sales Interview

Finally, there is the sales interview option. If you have a *limited number of prospects*, and want to make the most out of every single prospect, you may opt for this information delivery

---

[9]Bovee and Thill (1995), 97.

method. You realize that it is *more time consuming* (a **disadvantage for the salesperson**) but you take *no chance that the prospect will not give the information full consideration* (an **advantage for the salesperson**). You see to it personally that all questions are answered. You do not settle for the gain that comes from *symbolically* having multiple contacts with the prospect. You *literally* have these contacts.

Nevertheless, you must make certain that the sales interview is *convenient for the prospect*. If **your office** is not conveniently located, you must offer to come to **the prospect's home** or to meet at a **convenient location**. You must find a **convenient time** to get together. You must persuade your phone prospect that s/he will be able to conveniently consider the additional information.

Once you have determined the method that will be most expedient and convenient for both your phone prospect and you, present the matter in your one-minute telephone call. The way in which I handle this in my market is as follows.

Mr. Smith?

Good. Mr. Smith, this is Dr. Lindsay with the College Benefit Program. Would it be possible for me to have just one minute of your time today? Thank you.

Mr. Smith, we are sending free audio recordings to the seniors and graduate students who will be finishing up within the next 12 months and I understand that you will be finishing in May of [such and such year]; is that correct? Good.

The audio recording takes only about 17 minutes to listen to, but it provides information on how to save $1000 per year on your new car payments, how to earn the equivalent of almost 7 percent guaranteed interest on your savings (as compared to a taxable investment such as a bank CD), a better retirement program than an IRA, various insurance benefits, and free financial planning advice.

We're calling before we send the audio recording to make certain that you will have 17 minutes to listen, sometime within the next week. Will that be convenient for you? Good.

I have your address as [such and such]. We'll be dropping the recording in the mail right away. When you receive it, we ask that you listen as soon as possible, but at least within the next week, and then, if you will, just give us a call and let us know if you are interested in any of the benefits of the program, okay? Great. Would you prefer to receive your recording on a CD, jump drive, or an email attachment? Very good.

Your recording will be arriving in a day or so. Thanks for your time. Good-bye.

Once the phone prospect agrees with the premise of this sale, **the phone prospect becomes a full-fledged prospect**. You are ready to move on to the next group of sales.

Sale Number Nine brings us to implications in the Marketing Communication option called **Direct Marketing**. Technically, Direct Marketing occurs *when companies distribute their products and services to consumers without the use of a middle man* (a reseller, including wholesale and retail operations, and even salespersons). Nevertheless, Direct Marketing aims at **optimization**, typically the use of search engines to analyze consumers' behaviors according to **database information**, in order to detrermine to whom the companies should send their Direct Marketing communication. While the **salesperson (in Personal Selling)** should have similarly used any such information at his/her disposal, this optimization becomes **even more optimized** as the salesperson secures a *commitment* from the person to whom the material is being sent that *that individual will review the material* being sent.

Remember, however that **Personal Selling is NOT Direct Marketing**. Direct Marketing may well use the *telephone*, *printed material*, *CDs*, *DVDs*, *websites*, *email*, *podcasts*, and other technologies mentioned in Sale Number Nine, but *for the salesperson*, these methods are only an **intermediate stage** in the sales process. In *Direct Marketing*, they are the methods that are designed to **complete the sale**.

One may, instead, more accurately **compare the next three sales** (in the twenty-one sales) to a **very highly targeted form of Advertising**. Advertising has a variety of objectives. One might consider the **Advertising objectives of these sales**:

- *To persuade the prospect that s/he has a problem or need,*

- *To persuade the prospect that I have the necessary qualifications to help,* and

- *To persuade the prospect that my proposal is worth considering.*

These are all objectives that may be met by advertising—thus, saving precious sales time for the salesperson. This is the **true advantage of Advertising**: *If some of the twenty-one sales may be accomplished by mass communication, they should be.* As you consider the remaining sales in the twenty-one sales, as they pertain to the product or service you are marketing, you should analyze your IMC choices. If some sales are better accomplished by forms of Marketing Communication other than Personal Selling, handle them that way!

TWENTY-ONE SALES: PART THREE

AUDIENCE = PROSPECT

SALE NUMBER TEN

You Have a Problem/Need

Subject: Your problem/need.

Theme: Proofs of your problem/need.

Proposition: There are proofs that you have a problem/need.

Interrogative: What?

Key Word: Proofs.

Audience: Prospect.

Objective: To persuade the prospect that s/he has a problem/need.

Divisions: (i.e., "proofs")

1. The problem exists

2. You are a member of a class of people experiencing the problem.

Now that a specific prospect is willing to consider information on the matter that you wish to discuss, it is necessary to take the proposition of **Sale Number One** (*There are proofs that a problem exists*) and **apply it to the specific prospect**. It is *not sufficient* to prove to the prospect that *some* people have a problem or need. You must persuade the prospect that **s/he personally has the problem** or need. Conversely, it is *not necessary to reinvent the wheel* with this sale, either. You should return to **Sale Number One** to find those facts, statistics, authorities, anecdotes, case studies, and scenarios that you used **to convince yourself** that a problem or need exists. The job in **Sale Number Ten**, however, is to use **audience analysis** as you apply the proofs. Some of the facts and statistics that convinced you that a problem exists may not apply to your prospect. For example, in my market, I might relate to my (college senior) prospect the fact that "everybody dies sooner or later." S/he **may agree with me** (based on this fact) that a problem exists, but **might not consider himself/herself a member of the class of people experiencing the problem**. The prospect may view this as a problem which old people encounter. I must choose from my available proofs of **Sale Number One** those proofs that will be most salient to my audience of **Sale Number Ten,** my prospect. There are, thus, **two proofs** that I must offer to support my proposition **that s/he has a problem/need**. They are: (1) *The problem exists*; and, (2) The *prospect is a member of a class of people experiencing the problem.*

The Problem Exists

When I sold myself on the proposition that the problem exists in **Sale Number One**, I did not worry much about the organization of my sales presentation. I simply became involved with what is called **heuristics** or **invention**. Many are not familiar with the term *heuristics*, but are familiar with the related term *eureka*. I refer to the term as it was used *in the Gold Rush*, not the vacuum cleaner. The **"eur"** in both terms means **"to find."** When a prospector found "gold in them *thar* hills," s/he shouted, **"Eureka!" (meaning "I found it!")**. This is precisely what I did in **Sale Number One**. I did the research to find the proofs that were available. **Now, I am ready to organize my findings**.

The Greeting

Since I use audio recordings to supply the information for this sale, I personalize the recording at the very beginning, thus: *"Hi, Bob! Congratulations on reaching this stage in your educational career at [such and such] University!"* It may not be **wise in most markets to use Bob's first name,** here. I do, because, by this time, Bob has received my mailing with the letters Ph.D. on the return address of the envelope. Bob has read the cover letter with my signature above my name which is again followed by these letters. In the recording, **I will refer to myself as Stan**, but clearly Bob knows, by now, that I have some expertise. **Professors will typically address students by their first name. So, I address Bob by his first name.**

The Story

Following the greeting, I tell a story. I could tell an *anecdote*, a story about myself. I could tell a story about a particular *case study*. I could tell a scenario, a story that is fictional, but true to life. Frankly, *the story that I choose to tell contains a little of each of these*, but it is closest to the **scenario**. It is the **story of Bob**. I *never mention his name again in the recording*, after the greeting, because the rest of the recording is dubbed onto Bob's recording from the master recording that I have created. *Instead of the term "Bob," I use the term "you."* Having completed my market research, I know Bob's story fairly well. I *use statistics and personal experience* to describe what is currently happening to Bob. This is what I say:

> *By now, you may finally be able to see the light at the end of the tunnel! You see, most people never even come close! Only one out of three American citizens holds a bachelor's degree! Your job prospects, even in times of economic downturns, will be much better than those without the college degree. And, financially, statistics show that you will earn 66 percent more income in your lifetime than the high school graduates of your generation.*

> *But, it has certainly cost you to get to this point! How much? Probably in excess of $200,000, altogether! Just think. The average costs of going to college this year are over $25,000. Multiply that times four years of college, and you have already spent about $100,000! In addition, you have given up four years of your life. If you had been working at a decent factory job for those four years, you could have earned at least $25,000 per year . . . times four years. That adds another $100,000 to the price tag of your college degree!*

> *Yet, you'll tell yourself a thousand times throughout your life, "It was worth it!" You see, maybe without realizing it, you have become a major investor in the last few years. You have invested at least $200,000 in your head!*

> *If you had invested your $200,000 in new cars, four years ago, those cars might have a resale value today of only $80,000. If you had hidden your $200,000 in a hole in the ground, some thieves might have discovered it and stolen it. Even if they didn't, inflation would have eaten away at your value, until your money would be worth much less than $200,000, after inflation.*

But, you invested in your head! What are the chances you could lose that investment?

- *Well, the university could close down, and cancel every degree that it has ever awarded! And, your college degree would be worthless. That's not very likely.*

- *Some insane terrorist group could use atomic weaponry on us, and destroy all civilization as we know it. However likely that may be, there isn't much you and I can do to avoid the risk, so I'm not going to worry about it.*

- *Or, you could become involved in an automobile accident. Now, that's a possibility! What would happen, then?*

  1. First, you might be laid up in a hospital for weeks or months. The last time my wife was in the hospital for three days, it cost $40,000. Could you afford a long hospital stay?

  2. Second, you could become disabled. Perhaps your injuries would be so severe that you couldn't go back to work to earn an income. In that case, your entire $200,000 investment would be wiped out in a matter of seconds. If your college degree does not help you earn an income, why did you invest the $200,000?

  3. Third, you could be killed in the accident. My wife lost a brother and a sister to two automobile accidents, one year apart. Her sister was a student at Purdue University. Her brother was a student at Indiana State University. Statistically, out of this year's graduating class here at this University, one of you will die every single month for the next few years, and then the odds will rise to two per month, then three, then four, going up exponentially the older you get.

Note that, in my **scenario**, I use **facts**, **statistics**, and **anecdotes**. Yet, the story I have told is Bob's story. **By using scenario, I have made Bob the main character in the story**. It is Bob who sees the light at the end of the tunnel. It is Bob who is receiving a college degree. Bob will have great job prospects. Bob will earn much more money than high school graduates, because Bob has invested $200,000 in his head. Bob has given up the possibility of working full-time in order to go to college. **It is Bob's investment in himself that is at risk.** Bob's greatest risk might be an **automobile accident**. It would be Bob, laid up in a *hospital*. Bob could become *disabled* or Bob could *die.* How do I know Bob's story? *I know it because of facts, statistics, authorities, anecdotes, and case studies.* I know it because Bob is a member of a **class of individuals** who share pretty much the same story. I have done the **market research** in order to know.

You Are a Member of a Class of People Experiencing the Problem

Bob has just taken a **roller coaster ride** with me. We have *traveled back four years* in time to see the options that may have been available to him as a *high school graduate.* We have seen him *graduate from college* and I have *whetted his appetite* concerning the *rewards of this journey.* Then, we took a *side road,* and Bob wound up *wounded, disabled, and eventually dead.* Bob probably *did not like the end of this story.* But, I will not take the ending away, just yet. When Bob chose to take the ride, he agreed to see where it would lead.

I **started** the story **happily** for Bob. He probably would have stopped playing the recording immediately if I had started as follows: *Hi, Bob. Let's imagine that you are dead.* This is far too heavy a thought to begin the story but, somehow, *since this is the problem which Bob may have, I need to get there eventually.* The **contrast between the brightness** of Bob's anticipated career success **and** what could happen with an **unanticipated automobile accident** *shows the accident to be that much more severe of a problem.* When I use **narrative** to make my point, Bob is *not able to object easily.* I am telling the story. Bob is listening. **I am using entelechy**, implicit rhetoric. Bob is experiencing **identification** with the story. This is *quite overt identification.* The story is about *Bob.*

Now, however, I must **shore up the narrative with evidence** that Bob is actually a member of a class of individuals experiencing this problem. I have tried to interweave many **statistics, facts,** etc., into the fabric of the scenario. If I have **further important evidence** to offer which will not fit neatly into the narrative, I should **offer it following the story.** I might tell Bob that **automobile fatalities are the most likely killers of individuals in his age group.** I might **ask him if he knows of anyone close to his age who has died in an auto accident.** My guess is that **Bob will be able to help me provide anecdotal evidence**, here. Furthermore, <u>since Bob is</u>

relating the anecdote, he holds tremendous *ethos* for himself. I might share more of **my own personal knowledge of how such accidents affect the families** of the victims. I might talk about the *effect of such events upon my wife and her parents*. In my market, however, I also want to **be careful not to overdo it**. Most of my clients will actually use the *living benefits* of life insurance, *not the death benefits*.

Clearly, I must establish, before moving on, that *Bob has a problem*. If I fail to make this sale, the solution for the problem becomes irrelevant.

In IMC, using the **APIC decision sequencing model**, the **A** stands for **Analysis**. In proving that a problem exists, we are performing **situation analysis** before we move on to **causal analysis**, and finally, to **solution analysis**. We complete **all three of these analyses** before we move to the **P** in APIC: **Planning**. In business, **SWOT analysis** is the most common *situation analysis*. In SWOT analysis, we attempt to analyze the *Strengths, Weaknesses, Opportunities, and Threats* of a company. The **negatives** (**Weaknesses** and **Threats**) are things we may characterize **easily** as **Problems**. But, even Strengths and Opportunities (the **positives**) can be the basis for recommending sales. For example, if the company Say Press has a **Strength** (since it holds the copyright to the only expansive Kenneth Burke concordance in existence) and if there is an **Opportunity** (since there are over 1000 universities where Burkean studies are taught), an salesperson could sell Say Press on the existence of a **Problem/Need**: *You **need** to find a way to market this product to the libraries of those universities*.

SALE NUMBER ELEVEN

I Am Well-Qualified to Help You

Subject: Me.

Theme: My qualifications (or: Qualifications of Me)

Proposition: I/we have the necessary qualifications to help you.

Interrogative: What?

Key Word: Qualifications.

Audience: Prospect.

Objective: To persuade the prospect that I have the necessary qualifications to help.

Divisions: (i.e., "qualifications")

    1. I have expertise, and am associated with a respected business entity.

    2. I have ethics, and am associated with an ethical business entity.

This sale **must be made at this juncture**. Humility is a virtue, but **if you are too humble, people will not feel safe** enough to follow your **advice**. The trick is to fit this sale in comfortably, **minimizing** the possibility of it being interpreted as **boasting**. As one aspect of my proposal, I offer **free financial planning advice** for my clients. I use the occasion of mentioning this free advice **as an entree to an explicit presentation of my** *ethos*.

Sale Number Eight deals with initial *ethos* and its two elements--*prior reputation* and *first impressions*. This earlier sale of **initial *ethos*** is a largely **implicit** sale. By contrast, **Sale Number Eleven** presents matters **explicitly**. This presentation of *ethos* is close to what public communication specialists Neher, *et. al.* (1994) call **derived *ethos***. According to Neher, *et. al.*,

"Derived *ethos* refers to *the audience's impression of the speaker's credibility during the delivery of the speech. . . . The audience makes judgments about the speaker's credibility based upon the speech's content and delivery*" (p. 252). Since these comments about myself are made as part of the content of the recorded message, and come after the phone conversation, they constitute a form of derived *ethos*.

Another way of classifying *ethos* is by considering how the *ethos* was acquired. Thus, I distinguish **two types of *ethos***, *implicit* and *explicit*.

In our culture, offering an **explicit account of one's *ethos* is frowned upon**. The pertinent terminology (*boasting* or *bragging* or *conceit* or *pride* or *tooting your own horn* or *patting yourself on the back*, etc.) definitely carries a **negative connotation**. Nevertheless, **this sale must somehow be made**. If you were to deliver a **speech**, someone else might do the dirty work for you in a **speech of introduction**, prior to your standing up to speak. The individual giving the introduction could brag on you shamelessly. You could step to the lectern with great humility and thank the one who introduced you for such extremely generous words. You might even deny the full truth of the exuberant introductory praise, but the dirty deed would have been done. You would have been granted explicit *ethos*. If you write a **book**, someone might praise your work **on the cover**. The deed would be accomplished. But, how do you go about praising yourself? This is tricky business. **You could end up damaging your *ethos* by violating the no boasting rule**.

You could appeal to the fact that even Bible heroes, Jesus and Paul, defend their own credibility, but this might backfire, as well. Listeners might think, "So, now, s/he thinks s/he's in a class with Jesus and Paul?" It's a difficult task. **Here's how I put it:** *Last, but not least, we will provide you with free financial planning advice, throughout your career. This benefit is only as good as the professionalism of the one making the offer, so let me give you my credentials.* What are my credentials? They are two--I have **expertise** and I have **ethics** (but I don't explicitly state these two terms).

I Have Expertise

I borrowed my technique from a speech given by **John Savage**. I use a **general to specific** approach in the presentation of my expertise credentials:

> *There are over 1,000 individuals in this area who are licensed to offer the type of financial advice that I am licensed to offer.*
>
> *Out of these 1,000, only about 320 of us are college graduates.*
>
> *Out of these 320, only about 25 have been consistent members of the Million Dollar Round Table for the past several years. This represents the top 3 percent of the professionals in the industry.*
>
> *Of those 25, only one holds the Ph.D. degree and has completed the coursework for two other Ph.D. degrees, and you are listening to him on this recording.*

Savage's system works quite well. The **general categories are arbitrary**. The **differentiae are arbitrary**. You can choose those differentiae that will be most persuasive in identifying yourself as the top of a hierarchy, even if **the hierarchy is of your own making**. Kenneth Burke (1966) claims that humans are "goaded by the spirit of hierarchy (or moved by the sense of order)" (p. 16). Humans are forever creating new hierarchies. One might call **the hierarchy that I have identified** the **"doctorally-educated, historically high-producing, hierarchy of licensed insurance agents who are college graduates**." But this would miss the pragmatic (and dramatic) effect of following Savage's system. It **will work for nearly anyone**, and it is a **pleasant way to introduce one's expertise credentials**.

Not only will the system work **for individuals**, it is a nice way to move **one's company** out of the pack, **as well**: There are 2,150 eating establishments in the city of Metropolis. But of these 2,150, only 135 specialize in Italian food. Of these 135, only 12 deliver to your home. Of these 12, only one guarantees delivery within 30 minutes and we're the one. We humans love a good hierarchy!

I Have Ethics

When I explained *ethos* in the **Introduction** of this book, **I identified the two elements of** *ethos* **as expertise and active goodwill**. Why do **I here shift the phrasing of the second**

element from active goodwill **to ethics**? I guess it is just an accommodation to that nagging little voice inside me that says I am being somewhat disingenuous if I claim that (as a salesperson) I do not have **some level of self-interest** that might be **at odds with totally altruistic** motives. I do, in fact, have active goodwill toward my prospects, but **I also have active goodwill toward myself**. At times **these two properties** of active goodwill **are in conflict**. Hence, for the protection of my prospects, I practice *ethics*.

Webster's defines "**ethics**" as "*the discipline dealing with good and bad and with moral duty and obligation*." I find in this definition no implication of active goodwill, only good, moral behavior based upon duty and obligation. I feel fairly comfortable in claiming this for myself: I do have ethics. In my (recorded) sales presentation, I use **my reference to my graduate studies as a springboard into my explicit presentation of my ethical stance**:

> *I received my bachelor's degree from Lincoln Christian University, in Lincoln, Illinois, my master's degree from Indiana University at Bloomington, and my Ph.D. degree from Purdue University in West Lafayette. I have also completed all of the coursework for a Ph.D. at the University of Illinois in Champaign-Urbana.*
>
> *As you might assume from my undergraduate work at Lincoln Christian University, I am a Christian. As a Christian, I try not to treat anyone in a way that I would not appreciate being treated myself.*

I have identified the **Golden Rule** as the goal of my ethical behavior. I have identified myself as a Christian, and this term alone conveys a message of a complete moral code. In other words, there is an implicit moral code that Christians follow. I want to be **very careful**, since I have claimed the *ethos* that comes from being a Christian, **that I do not behave hypocritically**. I certainly do not want to bring discredit upon Christianity. This is not just a moral issue; it is a religious issue.

I also run the **risk that some of my prospects will have an adverse reaction to my identification of myself as a Christian**. Some may be Jews, some Muslims, etc. Some may even be atheists. Therefore, I phrase the basis of my ethics as the Golden Rule. I do not **explicitly** call it the Golden Rule. Frankly, the **Golden Rule is found in the ethical systems of many cultures and religions**. If someone does not value my Christian designation, it is still entirely likely that s/he appreciates the ethics of the Golden Rule.

For me, **the question becomes**, "How would I appreciate being treated, if I were in my prospect's shoes?" Here are a few of my **answers to myself**:

1. I would like the salesperson to be **honest**. If s/he makes an *honest mistake*, it is forgivable. If s/he *intentionally lies*, it is not. I will be the judge of his/her expertise. If s/he does not have the expertise to provide the best answer, it is my responsibility to determine this possibility.

2. I would appreciate **full disclosure**. I *do not like* to make *uninformed decisions*. I should be fully informed by the time the sales presentation is over. If *important details are left out* or (worse) *intentionally concealed*, I have not been treated ethically.

3. I would want evidence from **reliable outside sources** that I can trust the company that is providing my product. I know that I can check with the *Better Business Bureau*, on my own, but are there other industry rating services that are important for understanding the strength and ethics of the company? (I mention, on the recording that, while several different companies provide various parts of the program that I will put together for them, every one of these companies is ranked among the safest in America by *A.M. Best*, an independent rating service.)

4. I would appreciate **forewarning**. If I must **make a decision** within a specific period, I want to know about it.

5. I would like the salesperson to **respect my decision**, once it is made. I hate it when salespersons keep hanging on, trying new closes. If I have not been persuaded by the time decision-time comes, the salesperson should *graciously allow me to decline*.

6. I would appreciate a **friendly and respectful attitude** on the part of the salesperson, **whether or not** I purchase the product.

When I say I try not to treat anyone in a way I would not appreciate being treated myself, **I attempt to view the sales encounter from the prospect's perspective.** If you and your company **follow the suggestions in this book**, and cover all twenty-one sales, **you are being ethical**. In *Making offers they can't refuse*, I advocate **honesty** both intrapersonally and interpersonally. By covering all twenty-one sales, there is a good probability that there is **full disclosure**. Certainly, the company should fully disclose the *financial strength and reliability* of the company by outside rating service(s). In the process of making **Sale Number Thirteen**, there is **forewarning** that a decision is expected by a certain point. Also, throughout the *ethos* sales, a **friendly and respectful attitude** is being presented. This approach to selling is an ethical approach.

Company credibility (as well as **your own credibility**) can also be **enhanced by Public Relations** approaches. The implied "third party endorsement" of "good press" is useful in establishing the reputations and expertise of you and your company.

SALE NUMBER TWELVE

I Have a Proposal Worth Considering

SALE NUMBER TWELVE

I Have a Proposal Worth Considering

> **Subject:** Considering my proposal.
>
> **Theme:** Reasons for considering my proposal.
>
> **Proposition:** My proposal is worth considering.
>
> **Interrogative:** Why?
>
> **Key Word:** Reasons.
>
> **Audience:** Prospect.
>
> **Objective:** To persuade the prospect that my proposal is worth considering.
>
> **Divisions:** (i.e., "reasons")
>
> 1. My proposal will solve the problem
> 2. My proposal has benefits beyond problem-solving
> 3. My proposal is of the variety recommended by experts
> 4. My proposal compares very favorably with other solutions
> 5. My proposal is feasible

Before you actually present the proposal, you should attempt to **place the proposal in a positive light**. The actual proposals which you make to specific decision-makers may vary in detail. You should **not** attempt at this point (especially on a dubbed recording) to **provide the details of your proposal**. *Your prospect has not yet agreed to become a decision-maker!* You must **wait until you are speaking to a decision-maker** before you offer a proposal. However, you must offer enough of the "bells and whistles" of a proposal to **make your prospect believe it is worth his/her attention**. You must sufficiently entice the prospect to **make him/her willing to become a decision-maker**. **Sale Number Twelve** is not designed to sell the proposal; it is designed to **sell the notion that you have a proposal worth considering**. **Why** is your proposal worth considering? There are **five reasons**. Let's consider the first reason.

My Proposal Will Solve the Problem

Very superficially, you want to **outline what your proposal will accomplish for your prospect**. I will illustrate the point by using my own marketing example. Since I have identified three possible problems for Bob, associated with an automobile accident, I quickly present what my solution will accomplish:

> *This recording will provide information to you about some **fantastic benefits** that can help you become **financially secure throughout your career**. However, before we move on to the benefits, it only makes sense that we advise you on **how to make your first major investment secure** (that $200,000 you invested in your college degree).*

> *First, to **handle the doctor and hospital fees**, we can provide health insurance for you, if you need it. We know that, as soon as you begin working for a company, **the company will probably provide health insurance**. But, until you begin working (since your parents' insurance may stop covering you at graduation), you might need some **health insurance**.*

> *Second, to protect you against **the risk of disability**, we will set up for you a **retirement fund** that will **pay you $35,000 per year** (based upon current rates), starting at age 65, if you are permanently and totally disabled in the next few years.*

> *Third, **if you die**, we will **pay your family $200,000 income tax free**, to compensate for the cost of getting your college degree.*

Since, in **Sale Number Ten**, I had persuaded Bob that he has a problem, I want to make certain that **Bob knows that there is an available solution**. Yet, I do not want to belabor this point. I have let my prospect know that there is indeed a solution to his/her problem. Now, I want to *move past the negative motivation and on to the positive motivation.*

My Proposal Has Benefits
Beyond Problem-Solving

By telephone, in **Sale Number Seven**, my prospect is persuaded that the topic that I will be addressing is **relevant** to him/her. This relevance pertains to the problem(s) or need(s) which my prospect has. A **difference** exists **between the terms "problem" and "need."** Often the two terms refer to *different sides of the same coin*, however. If Bob has a *problem with doctor and hospital bills*, he **needs** *medical insurance* to pay the bills. If Bob has a *problem with an absence of income due to disability*, he **needs** some *disability benefits* to replace some income. If Bob's family has a financial *problem because Bob has died*, Bob **needs** to have a *life insurance benefit* to provide financial assistance to his family. Hence, I frequently *use the terms "problem" and "need" interchangeably*.

The term **"need,"** however, can have a **broader meaning** than "the solution to a problem." *Webster's* offers the following definition of "need": **"a lack of something requisite, desirable, or useful."** The lack of something requisite is fairly close in meaning to the terms "problem" and "need," used interchangeably. The *lack of something desirable or useful* **shifts the meaning** to a different arena. No longer does need connote the answer to a problem. Now, it seems **closer to a wish**.

In **Sale Number Seven**, I provide my phone prospect with a **list of needs** with which my business entity deals. In the example that I provide from my market, I list several needs that have little to do with a problem--how to **save $1000 per year on new car payments**, how to earn the **equivalent of almost 7 percent taxable interest on savings**, a **better retirement program** than an IRA. It is possible to translate these needs into problems, but I choose not to do so. These represent for the phone prospect *the "wishes" connotation of the term "needs."* Therefore, on the recording, I will expand on some of these wishes, in addition to solving the problems that I have noted. The following sample text is what I say, in my market:

Now, in addition to protecting your college investment, what else can we do for you?

*First, we will provide a **savings program that pays the equivalent of almost 7 percent taxable interest**. I'll explain later how this works, but it certainly beats a bank savings* *account that pays less than 2 percent taxable interest. You may use this part of the program as much or as little as you like.*

*Second, we will help you **save $1000 per year, on your automobile-related expenses**, for every new car that you buy and finance from now on. These savings alone, if reinvested with us at current rates, could provide **an extra hundred fifty dollars at age 65** for most seniors graduating this year. Let me explain.*

The average new car today has a sticker price of about $30,000. That sticker price includes about 10% to 20% profit mark-up for the dealer. This means that the dealer will probably make at least $3000 profit on every new $30,000 car that the dealer sells you at full retail.

However, there are some car buyers for whom dealers will offer to cut their profits to the bare bones. These buyers are often called "fleet buyers." They are frequently businesses, like car rental companies, who buy several new vehicles each year.

*What if you could buy cars like a fleet buyer? Instead of paying $3000 profit to the dealer on a typical new car, **you could save perhaps $2800 per purchase**. If you buy a new car once every three years, you would be **saving at least $900 per year**. Furthermore, if you finance those purchases, you might **save an extra $140 per year** (assuming a 5 percent interest rate) by not needing to finance that extra dealer profit. In addition, we can show you a way to **save an extra $100 or so per year** which 97 percent of the finance companies and banks would ask you to pay. Therefore, we can help you to **save well over $1000 per year on new-car-related expenses**. We teach you how to buy cars like a fleet buyer. If you like, you can reinvest your savings with us.*

*Third, we will provide a **retirement program with tax advantages** superior to those of an IRA.*

*Last, but not least, we will provide you with **free financial planning advice** throughout your career.*

Most products offer benefits beyond the sheer solving of problems. You as a salesperson must allow the prospect **not only to survive, but also to soar**. The prospect needs to dream, to envision future happiness, greatness, wealth, popularity, fame, accomplishment. You must **think**

of those additional "wish-needs" that the prospect may have which the product will help to provide.

My Proposal Is of the Variety Recommended by Experts

don't run down your industry to make yourself look better. you'll look bad)

I neglect the endorsements of my specific product at this point in the sales process. What I am after is a **transcendence of the product wars** that occur. There will be plenty of time later for comparing my product with those of my competitors. Many sales are lost because the salesperson is willing to **compete with close competitors at too early a stage**.

Burke's use of the term **"transcendence"** is as follows: "We mean by 'transcendence' the *adoption of another point of view from which [opposites] cease to be opposites.*"[10] When I begin the process of selling (in my case, financial products) by ripping all of my competitors (in my case, banks, insurance companies, etc.), **I lower the *ethos* of my entire industry.** There is actually **room for praising my entire industry**. *Why does it hurt* that there are thousands of institutions that attempt to *solve the problem that I am solving*? Does this not suggest that **everyone agrees that a problem exists**? True, I will eventually need to demonstrate that my specific product is the superior solution for my specific decision-maker, but, for now, I should *allow all of my competitors to help me gang up on my prospect*. What are the **industry-wide recommendations** for prospects? I will proceed with the illustration from my market. I continue:

> At the bottom, right-hand corner of the letter that I enclosed with this tape, you will see a triangle. Virtually **all financial experts** refer to this as **the financial triangle**. Notice that it is divided into **three layers**. The <u>bottom</u> layer is marked **"safe."** The <u>middle</u> layer is marked **"low-risk."** The <u>top</u> layer is marked **"high-risk."**
>
> This is your **first free financial lesson**. You need to build your financial future the same way you would build a house. You <u>don't start at the roof</u> and build downwards; you <u>start at the foundation</u> and build upwards. We provide a **basic $200,000 benefit**. This benefit is the foundation. It is marked **"safe."** Before you begin to invest in low-risk

---

[10]Kenneth Burke, *Attitudes Toward History* (Berkeley, Los Angeles, London: Univ. of California Press, 1984), 336.

areas such as mutual funds, there are four areas which financial experts encourage you to keep absolutely safe. I use an acrostic. I use the letters of the word **"s-a-f-e"** *to help you remember them.*

The letter **"s"** *stands for* **"sickness***.*** *You need* <u>health insurance</u> *to pay for doctor and hospital bills so that, if there is a special surgical procedure or medication or treatment that would save your life, they can perform it. The money will be there. If your sickness results in* <u>disability</u>*, so you can't go to work, you need* <u>an income</u> *to replace the income that you lost.*

The letter **"a"** *stands for* **"after 65***.*** *According to social security statistics, only 10 out of 100 Americans born 65 years ago are well-to-do today. We want to make certain that, when you reach age 65, you will be one of the ten.*

The letter **"f"** *stands for* **"fatality***.*** *When you are married and have a family, you will need at least ten times your annual income in life insurance. In other words, if you make $40,000 per year, you will need $400,000 in life insurance. For right now, we are providing just the first $200,000, to cover your college investment. You can provide the rest, later.*

The letter **"e"** *stands for* **"emergency funds***.*** *You need a savings account of some variety. Experts say that you should save up at least two or three months' income, in case of an emergency. It would be great if this emergency savings account were also earning the taxable equivalent of nearly 7 percent interest.*

Once we have set up the **"safe"** *level for you, you may consider yourself free to invest in some of the* **low-risk***, and, eventually, maybe even* **high-risk** *areas.*

<u>My Proposal Compares Very Favorably</u>
<u>With Other Solutions</u>

In the previous reason (for considering my proposal), I attempt to *transcend* the product wars. As I provide this reason, I actually attempt to locate a different type of business entity or product (which has previously earned respect) with which to compare my business entity or product. Far from attempting to put down another type of business entity, my **goal here is to build upon the**

favorable identification that the prospect already has with the <u>other</u> type of business entity. I want my prospect to view the transaction that is now transpiring in terms of a **favorable entelechy**.

In my market, quite candidly, insurance companies and insurance salespersons fight an uphill battle to regain respect. In **Sale Number Eight**, I make this observation: *"Every other salesperson who has ever **sold for the business entity** for which I am selling has affected the reputation of my business entity."* Here, I expand the statement: *"Every other salesperson who has ever **sold for the <u>type</u> of business entity** for which I am selling has affected the reputation of my type of business entity."* Nowhere is this claim more clearly demonstrated than in life insurance sales. In my career, I have had to pay the price for decades of obnoxious, inconsiderate, life insurance salespersons. This is not to say that the majority of life insurance salespersons are obnoxious and inconsiderate. Yet, there have been enough of them to make life difficult for the rest of us.

While some life insurance salespersons have been damaging the industry reputation, **another financial institution has garnered a certain level of respect**. I refer to the **banking industry**. True, there are stories of scoundrels in this industry, as well, but virtually everyone eventually settles upon a bank that s/he trusts. An individual *deposits his/her paycheck* in an account. S/he *applies for a mortgage* loan, car loans, etc. Bankers typically hold respect in town. Hence, when I attempt to provide a comparison of my financial proposal with another possible proposal, I elect to compare my proposal with a very respectable one. **I always point out, however, that the comparison that I am about to make is an analogy.**

I do **not** compare my proposal to the possible proposal of **just any bank**, either. I tell Bob (or whomever the recording is sent to): *"This is a comparison with **your** banker."* I want Bob to identify with me in the same way he identifies with his banker, not the unknown banker down the street. This is what I say:

> *I like to compare our $200,000 benefit with what your banker could do. This is an analogy. I don't know of any bankers who do what I am about to describe.*
>
> *If you went to your banker, and asked him to provide for you what our program provides, your banker could begin with the same basic premise that we begin with: You are already a major investor. You have already invested $200,000 in your head.*

Your banker might propose to you that, if you would invest a small amount of money with his bank, the bank (in return) would assume all of the risk of your first $200,000 educational investment. Let's say that he would take $200,000 of the bank's money and put it in a safe deposit box, in your name. Let's say that he would give you a written guarantee that, if you lose your life tomorrow, he will empty the safe deposit box and give the $200,000 to your family, free and clear.

Furthermore, let's say he would promise that, if you become permanently and totally disabled within the next few years, he would self-complete not only a $200,000 retirement fund for you, but a fund that could grow, at current rates, to over $1,000,000 in your lifetime, and give you permission to pull out money from your retirement fund along the way. I'm guessing that you would probably like your banker, wouldn't you?

Now, I don't know of any bankers who do that . . . free of charge, at least! If you know a banker like that, please, let me know, and I'll change banks. However, your banker could LEND you the money! If he gave you a $200,000 loan, at a 5 percent interest rate, you would be paying $10,000 per year, in interest alone! If he wanted you to pay off that loan over the next 50 years, he would ask you to pay an average of $4000 per year in principal! That could be $14,000 per year at first!

Forget that approach! We have a better idea. We will establish today, in your name, an estate worth $200,000. We will give you a written guarantee that, if you lose your life, we will pay that $200,000 immediately to your family. If you become permanently and totally disabled, we will continue to invest our money in your name for an entire lifetime. Your fund could be worth a million dollars, eventually.

Unlike the bank analogy that I made, we don't ever ask you to pay us back $200,000. We don't even use the terms principal or interest. We are not asking you to pay 5 percent per year. We do ask you to place a percentage of the $200,000 with us, but certainly not 5%. For most graduating seniors and graduate students this year, we are asking you to make a premium payment of only 1/2 of one percent per year! One half of one percent! It beats the dickens out of 5 percent plus principal!

Now, simple arithmetic tells you that ½ percent of $200,000 is $1000 per year. If you paid us $1000 per year, it would take you 200 years to pay us back $200,000. But, we don't expect you to live to be 220 or 230 years old. So, we're not asking you to pay that long. In fact, we are only asking most of you to pay that 1/2 percent per year for a period of only 30 years (at current rates)! That's a TOTAL CASH OUTLAY of only $30,000, instead of $10,000 or more per year in my earlier analogy.

To summarize, for that $30,000 outlay (about the price of a new car), you get $200,000 for your family, if you die tomorrow. You get a self-completing retirement fund, if you become permanently and totally disabled. If you need to get at your money, along the way, to solve emergencies, we make most of your $30,000 extremely liquid. We can usually get your money to you within one or two weeks of your request.

My Proposal is Feasible

The final reason a proposal is worth considering is that it is feasible. A particular proposal may solve the problem, have benefits beyond mere problem-solving, be of the variety recommended by experts, and compare very favorably with other solutions. However, unless the proposal is feasible, the prospect may not believe that it is worth considering. **The goal here is not to demonstrate exactly how it is made feasible**. The goal is simply *to allay those obvious feasibility fears* that the prospect may have. In my market, seniors and graduate students may not typically have an extra $1000 lying around. In fact, they may not be convinced that they will ever have that much extra cash!

I cover **two feasibility issues** for my prospects: (1) They **will have money later**; and (2) They **don't need money now**. Here is how I do it:

We'll help you save many thousands of dollars throughout your career on things like car purchases. This entire program, worth $200,000 in the different aspects, might be paid for by car savings alone! You might have all of these benefits without having to reduce your budget by a single dime!

*We also realize that not every graduating student has the money right now (while you are in school) to make payments right away. If necessary, **we can put off your payments** until you are **out of school** and earning an income. Then, you can begin cash outlays of*

$20 per week, or more or less than that amount, depending upon your financial situation. You see, we're not in the business of causing financial problems; we're trying to solve financial problems!

By this point, I have offered five good reasons for considering my proposal. Not every prospect will be persuaded to consider my proposal, but that does not mean that I have been unsuccessful at sales. **Thus far, I have completed eleven sales.** In my market, *I have not even met the prospect personally.* I have sold myself that a problem exists for which my product is a proper solution. I have persuaded myself that I am the right person to sell the solution. I have persuaded myself to do market research and to call my prospects. I have contacted many by telephone who agreed to give me a minute of their time. I have persuaded them that the matter about which I called is relevant to them and that I am engaged in a legitimate enterprise. They considered it worthwhile to consider more information on the subject. By audio recording, I persuaded many that they have a problem and that I am well-qualified to help them.

If they decide, at this point, not to consider my proposal, **I have not wasted any valuable sales interview time!** I will honor their decision and leave the matter behind. I believe that, even if they do not consider my proposal, **I have educated many college seniors** and graduate students concerning their need for financial planning. **I feel good** about that. I feel **ethical**. And, I have **saved my interview time** for only those prospects who are **seriously interested** in the matters that I have raised.

In **Sale Number Eleven**, I pointed out that Public Relations could enhance company credibility and your own credibility because of the implied "third party endorsement" of "good press." Another aspect of **Public Relations pertains to the giving out of free information**, with the *goal of gaining public **awareness** of your business*. The audio recording that is sent out to prospects contains a **free financial consulting session**, something that in Public Relations parlance amounts to "**news that you can use.**" By sending this recording, even if prospects are not interested in further considering my proposal at this point, I have engaged in useful Public Relations. Another area of Marketing Communication in which I have engaged is **Promotions**— "*providing opportunities . . . for "trying" the product now.*" The prospect, by listening to my audio recording has had the opportunity to "**sample**" my services.

SALE NUMBER THIRTEEN

You Should Agree to Become a Decision-Maker

Subject: Becoming a decision-maker.

Theme: Reasons for becoming a decision-maker.

Proposition: You should agree to become a decision-maker.

Interrogative: Why?

Key Word: Reasons.

Audience: Prospect.

Objective: To persuade the prospect that s/he should agree to become a decision-maker.

Divisions: (i.e., "reasons")

1. You will be more knowledgeable about this issue and this proposal when I finish than ever before and probably ever again.

2. This will provide better time management for all involved.

3. You will receive a written guarantee.

Although I personally try to complete sales prior to **Sale Number Thirteen** by telephone and audio recording, **I want the prospect in front of me for this most important sale**. As in **Sale Number Nine**, if my prospect agrees that it would be worthwhile to consider my proposal, I must *make certain that the sales interview is convenient for the prospect.* If *my office* is not conveniently located, I must offer to come to the *prospect's home* or to meet at a *convenient location.* I must find a *convenient time* to get together.

I may engage somewhat, here, in **social niceties** before we move on to the sales interview since this is our first face-to-face meeting, but I **prefer not to overdo the socializing**. Recall the **bank entelechy**. Bankers are polite and friendly, but prospects catch on to signs of *the buddy-up approach of salespersons*. In the mind of my prospect, if I behave like a salesman, this is a sales interview. If I behave like a banker/businessperson, **this is a business interview**. I prefer to **keep the entelechy businesslike**, bank-like. My time is valuable and so is the time of my prospect. S/he is here to consider my proposal, not to make a new friend.

Due to the fact that some **time has elapsed** since I called on the phone and since the prospect listened to the recording, I **review the highlights of what has been covered**, so far. I **use visuals** to **elaborate on the financial triangle and the "s-a-f-e" elements**. I verify that the prospect has comprehended **the analogy** and understands the type of proposal that will be presented. Then, I present the **proposition to the sale that is at hand**.

> *Now, I want you to feel free to interrupt me as we go through the details of your program. If there is something that you do not understand, just let me know and I'll explain it further. If I'm going too quickly, just say, "Stan, slow down!" Make sure you follow what is going on, so that by the time I finish going through the details, you will know everything you need to know in order to make an intelligent decision.*

> *It is **completely up to you** whether that decision is **"yes" or "no."** Whatever you say will be fine. The **one word** that we must **eliminate** from your vocabulary today, however, is the word **maybe**. When I finish going through the details, I need to ask you for a decision--either yes or no--whether you'd like to participate in the program. **Is that fair enough?***

Then, **I wait for an answer.** I want to make certain that my prospect affirms the fact that s/he has **agreed to change roles**. S/he is **no longer a prospect.** S/he is **now a decision-maker.** Frequently, the prospect will simply agree, at this point, to become a decision-maker. However, I am always somewhat skeptical of those who agree too easily. I **prefer those situations in which the prospect paraphrases** the agreement for me. S/he might say, "Wait. Are you saying that you want me to decide today whether or not I will participate in the program?"

My answer: **"When I finish going through the details, I have to ask you for a decision, either yes or no. Is that okay?"** Then I wait for an answer.

Frequently, the prospect will want to know **why I need an answer today**. I offer him/her essentially **three reasons**:

1. S/he will be more **knowledgeable about this issue** and this proposal, when I finish, than ever before and probably ever again;

2. This will provide **better time management for all involved**; and

3. S/he will receive a **written guarantee** that, if s/he can find, in the next two weeks, a less-expensive solution to his/her problem than this, we will cancel this purchase and refund all moneys paid in.

You Will Be More Knowledgeable When I Finish Than Ever Before and Probably Ever Again

There is **only one point in time** at which it is possible to make an **informed decision**--the **point at which one is most informed**. When the President of the United States needs to make a military decision, s/he calls in a team of advisors, experts from every necessary perspective. The President needs to know the whole picture before making a decision. Even so, there is no guarantee that the decision that the President makes will be the best decision, but it will be an informed decision. *Once the information is presented, the President will decide.* S/he will not wait until such time as s/he has forgotten the information. Frequently, the fate of the country rests in the balance. The **decision must be made, not delayed**.

Memory experts suggest that **forgetting** is a rather **rapid process**. It *begins as soon as we learn something new*. Although *I could repeat everything* that I have covered in the entire sales process, at a later date, the primary purpose for doing so would be to recall to memory those elements that have been forgotten. This *does not seem like a prudent use of time*. Instead, I make certain that all of the pertinent information is made available to the prospect at one time. This is **the single time in this person's experience when s/he will be the most informed** about the issue and my proposal. This is the **best time for the prospect to make an "informed" decision**.

This Will Provide Better Time Management

I tell my prospects that there are *more than 6,000 graduating students each year for me to contact*. I just **do not have time** to explain the program **multiple times to any given student**. For that matter, **the student** is probably in the midst of the **busiest year in his/her college** career. Not only are the *courses more difficult*, but there are also *graduation plans* that must be completed. There are *resumes to send, employment interviews* to keep. I feel fortunate that we were able to schedule this appointment at a convenient time, **as busy as we both are**. Rather than drag out the process, it makes sense to **be a good manager of time, now**.

Besides time, the only other *major quantity that requires efficiency skills* is **money**. I fear that, if someone is not capable of managing *time* efficiently, that person probably will not be capable of managing *money* efficiently, either. My goal is to make the person an efficient money manager. Benjamin Franklin even made the connection: "Time is money."

You Will Receive a Written Guarantee

My goal in asking someone to make a decision upon receiving all of the details regarding my offer is **not to encourage a bad decision**; it is to have the individual **make a good decision**. I have had prospects ask me, "What if I decide to participate in your program today, and then discover a better program tomorrow?" I consider this a **fair question**. It may represent the only piece of information that might be reasonably expected to be missing from my presentation. What salesperson would go through the process of persuading a prospect to purchase the product only to conclude with the comment: "By the way, you can buy a product similar to mine for 10 cents less across the street!"? Certainly, there is competition for sales. There may be other products priced for less than my product.

Perhaps, the price differential is insignificant. Perhaps, the issue is the credibility of the salesperson. I have addressed this issue to the best of my ability. The prospect should be able to make an informed decision concerning my *ethos*. Perhaps, the prospect wishes to know the strength and reliability of the company that I represent. I have addressed the issue. Perhaps, the prospect wishes to know if s/he really has the need for my product. I have addressed the issue. Perhaps the prospect wishes to know if the product is feasible for him/her. I will have addressed the issue. Indeed, **I have addressed every issue necessary for making an informed decision, except for a price comparison with every other company** offering a similar product.

In many cases, I could actually do that, as well, but the client may still harbor some lingering doubt. After all, I *am* a salesperson. It is my job to make my product look appealing. So, I give my prospect an **assignment**. I believe I gain more *ethos* by letting my prospect win this argument. I join in the argument on the side of my prospect. I **agree** that **more research** should be done. All other information necessary for making an informed decision will be presented today. All that will remain to be completed is **comparative price research**. I will **still ask for a decision**, but I **will provide a two-week guarantee**. The guarantee **describes my product specifically**. It states that, if the client can find **any other product like mine, available for a lower cash outlay** than that for which I have offered it to him/her, the one applied for will be canceled. Any **payments made will be refunded**. The client has two weeks in which to complete the research.

Despite these assurances, I occasionally have a prospect who refuses to become a decision-maker this day. If the person refuses to become a decision-maker, there would have been no possibility of completing a monetary exchange this day, anyway. I **do not throw the prospect away**. I simply point out what I said: "*When I finish going through the details, I need to ask you for a decision--either yes or no--whether you'd like to participate in the program.*" **We do not need to go through the details, *today*.** If someone else (a parent or a spouse) needs to be in on the decision, we will **reset the appointment**. If the prospect feels s/he must complete other preliminary research, that will be fine. The point is, **when we get together the next time, I will go through all of the details, answer all questions, and make certain that the decision-maker(s) is fully informed. Then, I will ask for a decision.**

Sometimes, the prospect decides to go through the details and make a decision, today. Sometimes, the prospect puts off the decision-making interview until later. Either way, my **Sale Number Thirteen** has been made. My prospect has agreed to become a **decision-maker**.

The sale that persuades the *prospect* to become a *decision-maker* is **unique to Personal Selling** among the forms of marketing communication. There is nothing in *Public Relations*, *Packaging*, or *Sponsorship* that comes near. *Advertising* can suggest that time is of the essence, but there is always a window of opportunity. *Sales Promotions* can offer a price break for a limited period of time, but there is still no requirement that the prospect become a decision-maker. *Direct Marketing*—especially in infomercials, sales "networks" (television channels devoted to selling merchandise), and similar commercials—has its "exploding deals" that last for only the next 10 minutes, etc., but that is **not the same as this sale**. They are **ultimatums**; this is a **sale**.

If the prospect understands why it is important for him/her to change hats and become a decision-maker, s/he has made a giant leap toward success. Virtually all humans are "considerers," but only a small percentage of humans are actual "decision-makers." These decision-makers run the world. They are the type of individual I prefer to have as clients. The decision will not always be in the affirmative, but no one's time will be wasted.

TWENTY-ONE SALES: PART FOUR

AUDIENCE = DECISION-MAKER

SALE NUMBER FOURTEEN

My Proposal Addresses the Cause of Your Problem

Subject: Addressing the cause of your problem.

Theme: Ways of addressing the cause of your problem.

Proposition: My proposal addresses the cause of your problem.

Interrogative: How?

Key Word: Ways.

Audience: Decision-maker.

Objective: To persuade the decision-maker that my proposal addresses the cause of his/her problem.

Divisions: (i.e., "ways")

1. My proposal determines the cause(s) of the problem

2. My proposal addresses each cause

Now that the individual sits in your presence as a **decision-maker**, you may analyze the cause(s) of his/her problem. You may return to the material covered in **Sale Number Two** as you were persuading yourself that your product is a proper solution to the need or problem. **Before you bring your decision-maker to the table, you should prepare your proposal.**

My Proposal Determines the *Cause(s)* of the Problem

Causal analysis begins by identifying **seven types of causes**: *immediate, perpetuating, remote, necessary, sufficient, hidden,* and *obvious.* The first place to look for potential causes of an increasing trend in a problem is what might be considered an **immediate cause.**

Immediate Causes

An *immediate cause* is a **coincidence**, a cause that comes into existence at almost precisely the same time the problem/trend begins (in other words, it **coincides with the beginning of the trend**). In the case of **correlations**, an immediate cause may be a trend in which the beginning to increase **correlates with beginning of the increase of the problem**. Hence, as I consider *coincidences and correlations*, I search for *immediate causes* of the **financial problems** associated with final expenses, hospital bills, and needs of dependents, pursuant upon the disability, hospitalization, or **early death of college seniors** and grad students, I must first list the **obvious immediate cause**: the college student's **death, hospitalization, or disability**. In considering **immediate causes** that may have caused the *death, hospitalization, or disability*, I might list such causes as:

1. Drinking and driving
2. Suicide
3. Drug overdose
4. Criminal activity
5. AIDS/HIV
6. Reckless driving
7. Skydiving
8. Private piloting
9. Serious illness
10. Not wearing seatbelts

In considering **immediate causes** that may have caused the *financial problems*, I might list such causes as:

11. No available emergency funds

12. No health insurance

13. No disability insurance

14. No life insurance

If some of the major causes of my decision-maker's problem are **any of the first six causes** listed, **I will not be able to help** that person financially. My product has a two-year exclusion for *suicide*, and, if there is a history of *attempted suicide*, the applicant will be declined by the company. Applicants will also be **declined** for a history of *drinking and driving*, *drug use*, *criminal activity*, *reckless driving*, *AIDS/HIV*, or *other serious illnesses*. These are not causes that will apply to those whom I will be able to help. These causes can certainly produce hospitalization, disability, and death, but, if someone identifies one of these as a cause, *our interview is over, for all practical purposes*. I tell decision makers that they may **pay for** insurance with *money*, but they **buy** insurance with *their health and safety record*. Once their health and safety record is damaged, they usually cannot get personal insurance at very affordable rates.

Sky diving and *private piloting*, while still somewhat risky, may not preclude my decision-maker from continuing with the interview. Typically, the company **will *provide** coverage, but **will exclude** from coverage any claims arising from these activities. Not *wearing seatbelts* is foolish, but it will not cause the decision-maker to be declined. I encourage my interviewees to *use wisdom to **reduce the likelihood*** *of a severe injury, disability, or death*, but there is no way to guarantee that such things will not occur.

Hence, **causes 11 through 14** comprise the major causes of the problem for my potential clients. All of these causes are *immediate*; they cause a problem at the precise moment when the accident, etc., occurs. When taken together in the right combinations, they are also ***sufficient*** and ***necessary*** for the problem to exist. My product/proposal will address these causes.

Remote Causes

A **remote cause** is a *prior, non-coincidental, non-correlating cause of a problem*. In the process of looking for immediate causes, via **statistical timelines**, and *correlating those statistical timelines* of the problem *with the statistical timelines of the prospective causes*, we may discover that some potential causes that we thought might have caused the problem were either **non-correlating trends** or **non-coincidences**. Some might suggest that **the lack of socialized medicine in the United States** may cause the financial problem students face. However, America **has never had** truly comprehensive socialized medicine. This is a **remote cause**. It began way back at the founding of our country. We may **reject** this *remote causes*. It has always been there. Some recent attempts to provide socialized medicine have been made, recently. But, even the Affordable Care Act does not automatically enroll college students in health insurance—and it has **no provisions whatsoever** for disability or death.

Perpetuating Causes

Three of the seven types of (or **ways of classifying**) causes are **time-related**: *immediate*, *remote*, and *perpetuating*. While *immediate causes* are causes that come into existence at almost precisely **the same time** the problem/trend begins, and *remote causes* are **prior**, non-coincidental, non-correlating causes of the problem, **perpetuating causes** are causes that did not come into play until **after the trend began**, but may have continued or increased the trend after it began.

One such *perpetuating cause* for the financial problem caused by the hospitalization, disability, or death of a college student is what my father-in-law and mother-in-law faced when Wanda and Larry died. It is the **psychological trauma** that **parents face** when their college-age children die. My father-in-law had earned an excellent income **before** his children died. He and my mother-in-law faced **severe depression and psychological crisis**. His **health failed**; neither he nor she could take the **stress** of even going to watch my wife, as a cheerleader, perform at high school sporting events. The events reminded them too much of Wanda's cheerleading days and Larry's athletic events. Their **financial picture plummeted**. He lost his good paying job, and eventually, **had to take much lower-paying positions**, as his health returned. I even wonder if **my father-in-law's aneurysm**, which took his life, was partially a result of this stress. His death at an earlier-than-anticipated time also produced **a further perpetuating cause** of financial problems for my mother-in-law. My father-in-law had not yet purchased any life insurance at the time of his death. These causes are *perpetuating* because **they began after** the problem began, yet **continued (or perpetuated) the financial problem**.

Necessary Causes

Without the necessary cause, there would be no problem. A **necessary cause** is *a cause, without which, the problem could never have started and could not continue*. The two types or categories of causes—*necessary* and *sufficient*—have one major difference from the three time-related causes—*immediate*, *remote*, and *perpetuating*. While a single cause (such as the death of the college senior) can be **only one of the three time-related causes**, it could theoretically be **both necessary and sufficient**. In other words, the death of the college senior cannot be both immediate and remote or both immediate and perpetuating or both perpetuating and remote. This is because the death existed *at a definite point in time*. It did *not* occur in the **distant past**, so it *could not be remote*. It did not occur in the **years following** the problem, so it *could not be perpetuating*. It occurred at *precisely* the **same time** as the problem began, so if it were a cause at all, it *would have to be immediate*. Since the **financial problems** associated with final expenses, hospital bills, and needs of dependents could not occur without the death of the senior, the death of the senior would be **both immediate and necessary**. **It is very helpful**, when arguing for the validity of one's causal analysis, **if one can locate a necessary cause**. And, if one can locate **a cause that is <u>both immediate and necessary</u>**, one has an **<u>extremely persuasive causal analysis</u>**.

The **only cause** we have identified that is **both immediate and necessary** is the **death of the college senior**. This cause *needed* to be present in order to have a financial problem pertaining to final expenses, hospital bills, and needs of dependents; therefore, it is a **necessary cause**.

Sufficient Causes

Earlier, it was noted that while a single cause (such as death of the college senior) can be **only one of the three time-related causes**, it could theoretically be **both necessary and sufficient**. It was also noted that, if one can locate **a cause that is <u>both immediate and necessary</u>**, one has an extremely persuasive causal analysis. Now it must be stated that, if one can locate **a cause that is immediate, necessary AND sufficient**, one has developed **the MOST persuasive causal analysis**. **Sufficient causes** *can cause the problem all by themselves.* In other words, they are "sufficient" to have produced the problem, even if no other cause were present. Since we have demonstrated that the **death of the senior,** is both an *immediate* and a *necessary* cause, ask yourself, is this cause sufficient to have produced a financial problem pertaining to final expenses, hospital bills, and needs of dependents all by itself? If the answer is yes, then we have an **immediate, necessary AND sufficient** cause. Since it is also an **obvious cause**, we have an **immediate, necessary, sufficient, and obvious** cause. (If, in some cases, one cannot locate a necessary cause for a problem, the **third most persuasive** cause is one that is **both immediate and sufficient**.)

Obvious and Hidden Causes

Obvious causes are clear and apparent to everyone. **Hidden Causes** are those that require more insight to discover; they are not apparent to everyone. Therefore, causal analysis argumentation is made considerably stronger, if one can identify and successfully argue that hidden causes exist. We have located an *immediate, necessary, sufficient, and obvious* cause, but are there any hidden causes that might be useful in our causal analysis? Perhaps the **perpetuating cause** (the **psychological trauma** that **parents face** when their college-age children die) would make our causal analysis even stronger.

Another Example

When doing causal analysis for any proven problem, you should **brainstorm** for a while, **listing all of the potential causes** of the problem that come to mind. For example, if the problem that you have identified is the decision-maker's recent *problem with getting his/her lawn mowed on a regular basis*, you might brainstorm the following list of causes:

1. S/he is working too many hours per day.
2. S/he is working too many days per week.
3. S/he is too lazy.

4. S/he does not own a lawn mower.

5. S/he owns a mower, but it is always breaking down, lately.

6. His/her lawn is too large to mow in a reasonable amount of time.

7. His/her grass grows too fast.

8. S/he doesn't care about his/her lawn's appearance.

9. His/her lawn mower is too small.

You might even make copies of the **complete list of causes** (I wouldn't call them excuses), and allow the decision-maker to mark all causes that might apply to his/her situation. You might leave a few blank spaces to see if the decision-maker can help *expand the list*. Let's say that the decision-maker marks numbers 3, 5, 6, and 9. This accomplishes some **causal analysis**. And, you know that *you do not need to sell this list of causes to the decision-maker*. S/he is the one who created the list. If you recall, from the **Introduction**, the discussion of **Socratic questions**, you have just used the technique. But do more. Try **analyzing the list of causes according to the categories of causes** which are used by Axelrod and Cooper (1994), and which are also discussed under **Sale Number Two**. From the cause list which you have just compiled, your analysis might be as follows.

Cause 3 (on the list) might be a *remote* **cause**, since s/he may have always been lazy. It is not a *sufficient* **cause**; it could produce the problem all by itself, but it did not cause it all by itself if the problem is a recent problem. It is not a *necessary* **cause**; one could have this problem, even if one were not lazy. It could be a *perpetuating* **cause**, since it might keep the problem going, once it begins.

Cause 5 seems to be more of an *immediate* **cause** than a *remote* **cause**. The breakdowns are probably occurring at the time that s/he is willing to mow; they have not always existed. The cause might be *sufficient*, since breakdowns could produce the problem all by themselves. It is probably not *necessary* for reasoning similar to that listed for cause 3. It could also be a *perpetuating* cause.

Causes 6 and 9 are *remote* **causes**--the lawn and the mower have always been the same sizes--unless I just purchased the home. If I just purchased it, the causes are *immediate* **causes**. They are also *sufficient* to cause the problem all by themselves.

When performing causal analysis, you apply the terminology as in the example above. Then, check to see which of the causes appear to contain **the strongest argument** in terms of being *immediate, sufficient, necessary,* **and** *perpetuating*. If you are selling lawn mowers, persuade your client that laziness is not a major cause of the problem. It may be *perpetuating*, but the other three causes seem to be *immediate* **and** *sufficient*. Perhaps, if lawn mowing did not seem like such a colossal task, the client might not feel as lazy.

My Proposal Addresses Each Cause

The *first way* my proposal addresses the cause of the problem is by **determining the major cause(s).** The *second way* my proposal addresses the cause of the problem is by **providing an element of my proposal to address each cause**.

In the *lawn mowing example*, the proposal should address each of the causes identified there. You might propose that the decision-maker *purchase a new mower* to reduce or eliminate the breakdown cause. Since the decision-maker cannot make the lawn smaller, s/he must make the *mower larger*. The enjoyment of operating a new mower that will make short work of the lawn job might reduce the feeling of laziness. The proposal addresses the cause(s) of the problem.

Since, in **my market**, the decision-maker does not yet have an **emergency fund**, we establish a fund for her/him. Since the student's **health insurance** may soon expire, we provide a quick and easy application for coverage. Since s/he has no **disability** or **life insurance**, we set some up. These elements **address the causes of final expenses, needs of dependents, etc.**, as well.

Many who attempt to solve problems provide only **"Band-Aid" cures**. They are like an incompetent physician who detects a skin infection and, rather than diagnosing the cause of the infection, simply covers it with a bandage. Physicians who practice thus soon lose *ethos*. Likewise, as a salesperson, **your responsibility to the decision-maker is to diagnose the cause of the problem before proposing a solution**. As a true professional, you need to make certain that you understand which causes have most likely produced the problem. Then, as a salesperson, let the decision-maker know that you have served him/her well in your diagnosis. Let the decision-maker know of the analytical process which brought you to your conclusion. Finally, show the decision-maker **explicitly** how your proposal addresses the cause of the problem

SALE NUMBER FIFTEEN

My Proposal Will Solve Your Problem

Subject: My proposal solving your problem.

Theme: Proofs of my proposal solving your problem

Proposition: There are proofs that my proposal will solve your problem.

Interrogative: What?

Key Word: Proofs.

Audience: Decision-maker.

Objective: To persuade the decision-maker that my proposal will solve his/her problem.

Divisions: (i.e., "proofs")

1. Authorities

2. Statistics

3. Case Studies

4. Anecdotes

In order to avoid "Band-Aid" approaches to problem-solving, it is necessary to complete **Sale Number Fourteen** before turning to **Sale Number Fifteen**. Once it is clear that your proposal addresses the cause of the problem, the decision-maker knows that you are attempting to cure the problem, not simply patch it up.

A handyman or a do-it-yourselfer is often one who specializes in patch-up solutions. I qualify as such an individual, as a practitioner of automobile maintenance. Once, years ago, I began to hear some rumbling under my car. I knew that the cause of the rumbling was a rusting exhaust system, but I patched up the problem rather than repair it. I did not address the cause of the problem. I slid under the car and noticed a hole in the exhaust pipe. I found a tin can, cut out both ends, and cut through one side. I wrapped the tin can around the exhaust leak and secured my patch with hose clamps. A month later, I heard the rumbling, again. My "Band-Aid" had either come off or it was a new leak. I continued to patch until my wife complained too loudly. Then, I took the car to a mechanic who replaced the exhaust system for me. For years after the exhaust system was replaced, there were no new rumblings. Amazingly, by addressing the cause of my problem, the mechanic actually solved my problem.

One could say, therefore, that **Sale Number Fourteen** is actually a part of **Sale Number Fifteen**. However, the sheer *fact that a proposal addresses the cause* of the problem is **no guarantee** that the proposal *solves the problem*. History contains many examples of individuals who had **addressed the cause of the problem of poverty at retirement**. The **cause** of the problem was that the **workers had not saved money systematically** throughout their income-producing careers. This cause was definitely *sufficient* to cause retirement poverty, and almost always *necessary* for the problem of poverty at retirement to exist. So, workers found solutions that addressed the cause. They found systematic money-saving solutions.

Unfortunately, these solutions did **not always solve the problem**. Some invested in *banks* and *savings and loans*, **prior to** the establishment of the Federal Deposit Insurance Corporation (FDIC) and the Federal Savings and Loan Insurance Corporation (FSLIC). When their **banks and/or savings and loans went under**, the workers *lost their savings*. Some invested in the *stock market*. When **it crashed**, they lost. Some invested in *company-sponsored or labor union-sponsored pension programs*. Various and sundry **theft schemes** ensued. Often, these programs were bankrupted.

I sometimes point out to decision-makers that, **even during the Great Depression**, funds held by **life insurance companies** that were members of the **various state insurance associations were safe**. Those who accumulated funds in life insurance company products were able to solve the problem. To say that my proposal will solve your problem is to say that **my proposal is not a temporary patch**. It is to say that my proposal **has longevity**. It is to say that my proposal incorporates **safeguards against failure**.

I once joined a *buyer's club*. The *problem* I faced was the *high retail cost of furniture*. The buyer's club allowed me to *purchase furniture for just a few dollars above the cost* to furniture stores. Two years after I paid a rather substantial membership fee, **my buyer's club closed** its doors. Fortunately, I had moved to a different city and had transferred my membership to a different buyer's club mere months before the closure. This new club served me faithfully for a few years. Then, I was informed that the club was *under new ownership*. I *had to pay more* to keep my membership active. The club began *requiring payment-in-full for merchandise before* ordering the merchandise. When this club went under, there were *many who had paid for merchandise that had not been delivered*. I was not one of them, fortunately. Now, whenever someone encourages me to purchase something upon which I will depend for some time**, I ask to see the warranty, the financial status of the company.** I want to know the **contingency plans**, should this company fail. I want to know that **the proposal will solve my problem**.

I need to sell my decision-maker on the proposition: "There are proofs that my proposal will solve your problem." I offer basically **four types of proofs**--*authorities, statistics, case studies,* and *anecdotes*.

Authorities

In **Sale Number Twelve**, I was content to *transcend the competition* in my industry. I *praised my entire industry* (as I did in this sale, concerning the *historical reliability of insurance companies* to protect funds). The same system that protected policy owners in the Great Depression is still in existence, today. It has protected policy owners whose companies have collapsed within the past decade.

However, prudence demands that I *not rely merely upon the industry safeguards* which are in place. I want my decision-maker to know that I keep an eye on the **financial stability of the companies I represent**. I provide *A. M. Best reports* on my companies. I do not recommend insurance companies with an A. M. Best rating lower than B+. I let my client know the difference between ratings, if one company offers a policy for less money but is ranked lower. **Authorities** are those *independent experts who provide ostensibly unbiased analysis of various products and companies*. I encourage my decision-maker to consider the expertise of the authority, as well. Sometimes, a popular magazine makes a recommendation that is quite naïve.

It is **ethical** to make certain the decision-maker is aware of the reliable analysts for the specific industry.

Keep in mind that the **objective of this sale** is: "To persuade the decision-maker that my proposal **will solve his/her problem**." The goal at this point is **not**: "To persuade the decision-maker **that my product is the cheapest**." Use those authorities that will support the claim that the proposal **will solve the problem**.

Statistics

Statistics connotes the use of **many numbers**. These may be *numbers of individuals whose problems have been solved by your proposal*. They may be numerical *demonstrations of the ways in which the problem is solved*. They may be *amounts of money paid out* in the past in order to solve the problem. They may be the numb*ers that demonstrate the financial stability of the company*, the evidence that the company will be around to keep promises.

These statistics are **not numerical proofs that the problem exists** *or* **statistical probabilities that the problem is relevant** to the decision-maker. Statistics were used for these purposes, earlier. **Here, statistics** are only used to persuade the decision-maker that the proposal **will solve his/her problem**.

Case Studies

While statistics and authorities can be persuasive, **case studies** *put "flesh and bone" on impersonal numbers*. This is a good place to give the decision-maker some **"real-life" evidence** that problems are being solved by my proposal. The company may have *testimonials*, *thank-you letters*, and *news accounts of real people* who were benefited by similar proposals.

Anecdotes

Of course, the type of real-life example that **contains all three of Aristotle's means** of persuasion (*ethos, pathos,* **and** *logos*) is the **anecdote**. If you know *from personal experience* that your proposal will solve the problem, let the decision-maker know. There is nothing more persuasive that the conviction of a person who relates **his own story**.

In 1987, I proposed to **my dad** that he needed much more life insurance than he owned. Dad was in good health. He had no reason to suspect that he would die until he had reached a ripe old age. But, what if he did? Mom would have to sell land quickly to pay the bills. Some of his children owed him substantial amounts of money. Could Mom prevail upon the kids to pay up at such a time? Yet, having loaned so much cash to his children, Dad did not have the cash flow at retirement to pay large insurance premiums. My proposal: Let's buy the insurance and have the kids who owe money pay most of the premiums.

Shortly after Dad qualified for the insurance, he became ill. The disease affected his kidneys. Soon, Dad was relying on dialysis. The procedures kept him alive for several years, but the inevitable day arrived. When Dad died, Mom and I placed a phone call to the insurance company. Without a moment's hesitation, they consoled us and said that all that was required was a copy of the death certificate. Within days, *large sums of money* came to our family *income tax free*. The proposal that I had made to Dad a few years earlier had **solved the problem**. *Mom* was taken care of. The *debts the children had incurred* to Dad were paid. My proposal solved the problem.

Sale Number Fifteen establishes the proposition: There are proofs that my proposal will solve your problem. Although **deductive** arguments may be advanced to support the proposition, the clearest and generally most persuasive proofs that a given proposal will solve the decision-maker's problem are **inductive**. These inductive proofs are multiple *examples* (with varying levels of *pathos*) of the fact that similar proposals have solved similar problems for others. Three **varieties of inductive proofs**/examples are **anecdotes** (personal examples such as my personal experience with my dad), **case studies** (examples which must be culled from research), and **statistics** (collections of numerous examples from which reliable conclusions may be drawn). The use of **quotations from authorities** to supplement these inductive proofs **adds *ethos***. The inductive proofs may be trusted. Credible sources support the conclusions.

Advertising Approaches to This Issue

Some **common formulas for Advertising messages** are used to make the sale that the company's **product will solve the viewers' problem**:

- **Problem solution/problem avoidance**

- **Slice of life**
- **Spokesperson/endorser**
- **Demonstration**, and
- **Comparison**

In *problem solution/problem avoidance*, the **product becomes the hero**. Tide ran an effective advertisement about its stain removal pen, in which an individual was being interviewed for a job. The interviewer, however, could not hear what the interviewee was saying because the stain on the interviewee's shirt kept interrupting—screaming out whenever the interviewee attempted to speak. The Tide pen comes to the rescue, as the hero. The Tide pen can remove stains on one's clothing in an instant. The job interview, in this case, can be rescued by the product. The **product solves the problem**.

Slice of life advertisements are common, as the camera appears to **"cut in" on a conversation** two people are having about a problem. One character complains that she or her husband or child, etc., has a problem with sleeplessness, hemorrhoids, snoring, acne, constipation, etc. The other character (usually, a friend) offers a friendly suggestion that she try the product, as a solution. In the final scene, the two converse again: the product was used; the problem was solved. The **product solved the problem**.

Actual *demonstrations* of the product show that the product works to solve problems. The side of the face untreated by the facial cream has more wrinkles than the side treated by the product. The area of carpet protected by the carpet treatment spray stayed cleaner after heavy traffic than the area left unprotected. The various **products solved the** various **problems**.

A *comparison* of the product with its competitors shows that the product is superior in solving problems. The laundry washed in the product looks cleaner than the laundry washed in Brand X. The fluid spilled in two identical areas is more quickly absorbed by the "quicker picker upper" paper towel. The preferred **products solved the** various **problems** in a fashion superior to their competitors.

If it becomes *difficult in a brief commercial advertisement to prove* that the product works to solve a problem, a trusted *spokesperson/endorser* may be hired **to supply** *ethos*. Wilford Brimley, Andy Griffith, and Fred Thompson are believed to have *ethos* for older citizens. Therefore, Fred Thompson endorses AAG for reverse mortgages. Andy Griffith endorsed many products—from crackers to cereals to coffe--in his younger days. When he was older, he was seen as a valuable spokesperson/endorser for ObamaCare. Wilford Brimley endorses Liberty Medical as a treatment for diabetes. These endorsers claim that the **products** they recommend **solve the problems**.

Marketing Communication practitioners agree concerning the importance of this sale. The audience needs to be persuaded that the product solves the problem.

SALE NUMBER SIXTEEN

My Proposal is Feasible

Subject: My proposal being feasible.

Theme: Criteria for my proposal being feasible.

Proposition: My proposal meets all the criteria for being feasible.

Interrogative: What?

Key Word: Criteria.

Audience: Decision-maker.

Objective: To persuade the decision-maker that my proposal is feasible.

Divisions: (i.e., "criteria")

     1. You can afford my proposal

     2. My proposal can be implemented in a timely manner

     3. My proposal can be implemented easily

In **Sale Number Twelve**, I promised my prospect (by audio recording) that my proposal would be feasible. I did *not, at that time,* demonstrate exactly how it is made feasible. I saved that demonstration for this sale. Wise real estate salespersons will **not waste time** trying to sell expensive homes to individuals who **cannot afford** them. If the purchase of the real estate is not feasible, because there is no way the prospect could qualify for the financing, the wise salesperson will attempt to shift the attention of his/her prospect to something that is more feasible. One cause of the real estate crash that occurred from 2006 to 2012 is that the federal government had, in the **Community Reinvestment Act** (passed in the 1970s, then fortified in the 1990s), required banks to make loans to people with poor and nonexistent credit histories. Many of those who purchased homes, as a result of this act, could not afford them. The purchases were **not feasible**. Feasibility must be considered. Nevertheless, there is little point in talking in detail about the feasibility of purchasing something, *unless the decision-maker believes the purchase will solve his/her problem.* On the other hand, **salespersons who conceal all cost information until this point in the sales process lose** *ethos*. If the prospect or decision-maker wants to know (at an earlier stage) the price range of the proposal, I certainly let him/her know. I **provide the range**. My range is, however, large enough to encompass a number of alternatives. **Affordability** (price range and/or the ability of the decision-maker to pay the price) is the **first criterion of feasibility**.

You Can Afford My Proposal

I can accommodate a graduating student who cannot afford to pay a dime for the next year. I simply offer a low-interest rate **promissory note** for the year. The money that the student is borrowing is *actually placed in an accumulation account in the policy*. This account earns interest and also has the cost of insurance deducted, each month. If the student dies while the promissory note is unpaid, his/her family can use an extremely small portion of the proceeds from the policy to repay the promissory note. If the student becomes permanently disabled while the promissory note is unpaid, the company will pay additional premiums into the policy. The note can be paid by the policy itself. When the student graduates and begins to earn a living, premium payments and note payments can be included in his/her budget. If, four years later, the client becomes unemployed, the *premium payments are flexible*. The client may stop making payments for a while. Mine is a very *affordable* solution.

For graduating seniors and graduate students who are persuaded regarding the earlier sales in a sale, the feasibility sale is *where my proposal really shines*. Other companies that may be able to offer a product similar to mine are unable to offer the feasibility that my proposal offers. **Car dealers** have developed a very similar approach to selling new cars in this market. Once a college graduate produces a certificate of employment, Nissan dealers offer 100 percent financing and a three-month payment deferral plan. Other car dealers, Ford, GM, Chrysler, etc.—have offered similar deals in various years. This gives the graduate a chance to formulate a budget, after the initial expenses of establishing a home. I know personally that this is true. My son purchased a car from Ford and my daughter a car from GM, using this plan.

Although the deferred payment plan works for college seniors, it does not work as well in other markets. Simply delaying payments for one year for individuals who are struggling to make ends meet invites disaster, both for the buyer and for the seller/creditor (as in the housing market crash).

In some markets, affordability must be achieved **by saving money elsewhere**. Heating contractors often demonstrate affordability in terms of the fuel bill savings which result from owning an energy-efficient furnace. Washer and dryer salespersons may appeal to the savings netted by not using laundromats.

Sometimes, affordability is achieved **by computing the value of the decision-maker's time**. If the decision-maker is *able to spend more time producing income* by owning a new technology, etc., the added technology is viewed as affordable.

Sometimes, affordability is not a problem. If the decision-maker *wants something*, s/he gets it. We often find ways of affording what we really want.

My Proposal Can Be Implemented in a Timely Manner

The **second criterion of feasibility** pertains to time. Can this proposal be **implemented within a reasonable time**? If the decision-maker has a problem this very minute, *how long will it take for my proposal to take effect?*

If I am dying of hunger, will I wait in line to be seated at a nice restaurant? Will I drive through at McDonalds? If I have a splitting headache, will I call for an appointment with my physician? Will I just grab the bottle of aspirin on the shelf? I may appreciate the affordability of purchasing a new car through an auto broker, but how long will I have to wait for delivery? Will I pay more just because a dealer has a car in stock?

I am still selling my decision-maker on the proposition that **my proposal meets <u>all</u> the criteria for being feasible**. *Affordability* is only *one* criterion. *Timeliness* is the *second* criterion. In my market, I again have something to sell, here. Since other companies have no affordable way of setting up insurance programs for penniless college seniors, they are content to wait until the senior graduates and begins to earn an income. I, on the other hand, have "timeliness" on my side. **I can place tentative coverage in force the very day** I speak to an individual. I can *give the student a conditional receipt* for the *premium payment* by promissory note.

I once had my vehicle repaired by a close friend in another city. I knew that the repair would be *affordable* because my friend was the most reasonably priced mechanic I had ever done business with. Yet, *as the weeks turned to months, I realized that it was not very feasible to have my friend make future repairs for me.* The problem was *timeliness*. I needed to have my vehicle operating now, even if it meant the loss of some *affordability*.

My Proposal Can Be Implemented Easily

The **final feasibility criterion** is **ease of getting started**. For many products, this is not an issue. You simply pay your money and take your product. For other products, this is an extremely important issue. Consider technological sales, for example. The decision-maker may be able to *afford* the product. The product may be available for *immediate delivery*. The individual may be quite willing to purchase and use the product. Yet, *getting started* may be the kicker. When I bought my first personal computer (yes, way back when they first became available to consumers), *I attended a computer school full-time for one week to see how to operate the computer*. Even so, there were many things that I did not understand. There were times that I needed a consultant to help me out of a jam. I still need one from time to time. I paid an exorbitant price for the computer—more than I paid for my new car, at that time. This meant that the technology produced an **affordability** issue for me. Nevertheless, if I had simply purchased the lowest-priced computer, even if it were a superior product, I would have experienced tremendous feasibility problems because I would not have known how to use the technology; whereas, by buying an IBM PC, through a source that provided the week-long training session, I found it **easy to get started** using my computer.

A decision-maker may be willing to purchase a bicycle from a department store, until it becomes an unfeasible purchase. The buyer discovers that s/he must assemble the thing himself/herself. A decision-maker may be willing to purchase a new sports car, but s/he may be unable to drive a stick shift. The purchase must be made feasible. It must be **easy to get started**.

In my market, **physical exams are required** for many purchases. These may be considered feasibility problems. We try to make these exams as **easy to accomplish** as is possible. *We contact* the *paramedical service. They*, in turn, *contact the client and schedule an appointment* to conduct the physical exam *at the client's residence and at the client's convenience*. Even so, occasionally, the decision-maker considers the physical exam inconvenient. Some decision-makers even fear needles. *If a decision-maker considers the physical exam a feasibility problem, I might recommend a smaller policy size.* In that case, the medical underwriting requirements may be different. The decision-maker might not need a physical exam. Regardless, there are always applications and promissory notes to fill out and sign. I try to have as much of the required information as I can researched in advance. I do not want to run out of time in the sales interview before getting all paperwork signed. I need to **make getting started as easy as possible**.

One criterion of feasibility is not sold to the decision-maker; but it **is of concern to the salesperson**. This feasibility criterion typically relates to **proposals for solving social problems**. Government has long *required seatbelts* for every car because they can save lives, but *feasibility* asks, "*Will the people* actually fasten their seat belts?" We may *propose a safer speed limit* of 55 or 65 miles per hour, but feasibility asks, "*Will people* drive at or below the speed limit?" We may propose that, for safety's sake, *bicyclists wear helmets*, but feasibility asks, "*Will people* actually do it?"

Even in an interpersonal proposal such as a direct Personal Selling situation, it is important to **ask yourself, "Will people do it?"** The best-priced, most secure life insurance policy in the world will not solve the problem *if the decision-maker will not buy it*. I must be candid, here. If I were cynical, I would say that **there is very little reason for a person to buy pure life insurance**. There is **not a good selfish purpose** for the product. Certainly, there have been times individuals have *made a cash outlay of as little as $10 and subsequently have died*. The company I represented has *paid out thousands of dollars* of benefits for that small cash outlay. Yet, **the person who purchased the insurance did not receive any of the multi-thousand dollar benefit**. The *person who purchased the insurance had died*. So, why did that person purchase the product? It was **not due to self-interest**. It was due to an **unselfish** consideration of someone else. In sappy language, the only word for such unselfish action is **love**.

Cynics believe that *no one is truly unselfish*. If that were so, *no one would purchase pure life insurance*. I will grant cynics one thing, however. I will grant them the fact that *many people are selfish*. There is always a feasibility question involved when certain products (life insurance, for example) are sold. The question is, **"Will the decision-maker** actually act unselfishly?" This is not a question of whether or not the product is the *lowest priced* or offered by the *safest company*. This is a question of feasibility that **pertains to human character**. Frequently, the decision-maker will use a **smoke screen** *to hide the basic character issue*. The decision-maker will claim that s/he *needs to compare prices or to check out industry ratings or to gain the advice of someone else*. What the decision-maker **actually means**, however, is *that s/he is too selfish* to purchase the product for some other person's benefit. The decision-maker does not want to admit to this truth.

I was taught a good **method for exposing this smoke screen** at a school that was administered by Fidelity Union Life Insurance Company. If the decision-maker contends that s/he just needs to check prices, I was taught to say, **"*Just suppose for a moment* that this was not a problem . . . "** (Today I expand upon the method: "*Just suppose that you were convinced that you had found the best-priced policy available*.") I was taught to continue, **"*Then, would you be interested* in purchasing?"**

If the decision-maker says, **"Yes,"** I know that it was **not a "smoke screen."** I would, then, move to the guarantee that I mention above: "*Very well, we give you two weeks to check into the price of any other product you would like to compare this with. If you can find a lower-priced product, we will cancel this policy and refund your money*." The decision can be made, today, **contingent upon the client's future price shopping results**. Likewise, if the decision-maker wishes to confirm the A. M. Best rating of the company on his/her own, the decision can be made **contingent upon the client's rating research**.

If, however, the decision-maker says, **"No,"** I know that the objection **was a smoke screen**. I was taught to continue, **"*Obviously, you have a reason for saying that. Do you mind if I ask what it is?*"** The decision-maker can then offer a different reason. I can *respond with the same* **"*Just suppose* . . ."** and continue this discussion **until we both discover the true reason**. All too frequently, in life insurance sales, the real reason for a negative decision is character. Some people simply will not do it. Some may be too selfish. If I have made the other sales, it is very probable that I have simply run into a feasibility sales obstacle. There is very little I can do about this. I *could use shame* to motivate a sale, *but I choose not to*. I do believe that it is **quite ethical to pinpoint the true reason** for the decision, however. I do not believe that allowing a smoke screen to exist benefits anyone. I believe in **honesty** on the part of both the salesperson and the decision-maker.

There are certainly instances in which a sales proposal is not feasible due to the selfishness of the decision-maker. Yet, if you as a salesperson persuade the decision-maker that s/he can **afford** your proposal and that your proposal can be **implemented easily** and in a **timely** manner, *you have done a great deal to persuade* the decision-maker that your proposal is feasible. Since your proposal *addresses the cause* of the problem, *will solve* the problem, and is *feasible*, you *may* have *already nearly persuaded* the decision-maker to *enact your proposal*.

In **<u>Marketing</u>**, the issue of financial feasibility is dealt with in one of the **Four P's** of marketing: **Price**. As a retailer, Sears deals with the price issue by offering three price (and corresponding quality) levels for many of their Kenmore appliances—**good**, **better**, and **best**. Companies marketing products may use **positioning according to price**. They may see that their competitors already have the market share with *medium* and *high* prices, but that the position available to them is the *low* price. These companies make the ownership of products more **feasible** for lower income consumers.

In **<u>Marketing Communication</u>**, the issue of feasibility is frequently the province of **Sales Promotions**, particularly **Consumer Promotions**. *Consumer* Sales Promotions offer consumers (often financial) incentives to purchase (*pull*) products. This makes the purchase of the products more feasible/affordable. (*Trade* Sales Promotions, on the other hand, offer retailers and wholesalers incentives to sell [*push*] products. While these Trade Promotion incentives, sometimes, trickle down to the consumer, they do not always do so.) The **granddaddy of Consumer Promotions**—the **coupon**—is an example of the way Sales Promotions make purchases more feasible.

SALE NUMBER SEVENTEEN

My Proposal Will Help to Solve Other Problems

Subject: My proposal.

Theme: (Other) Problems solved by my proposal.

Proposition: My proposal will help to solve other problems.

Interrogative: What?

Key Word: (Other) Problems.

Audience: Decision-maker.

Objective: To persuade the decision-maker that my proposal will help to solve other problems.

Divisions: (i.e., "problems")

    1. Problem One.

    2. Problem Two.

    3. Problem Three.

    4. etc.

This sale is optional, but, **if you have something to sell here**, you should certainly **sell it**! This part of the sales process is pure **icing on the cake**. The decision-maker has seen that the proposed solution to his/her problem addresses the cause of the problem, will solve the problem, and is feasible. **This sale will solidify** what the decision-maker already wants.

Suppose an **exercise-equipment** salesperson has proposed an equipment purchase in order to help the decision-maker lose weight. *Excess weight is the primary problem* being solved. The salesperson has considered the two basic causes of a weight problem--excessive caloric intake and too little caloric expenditure. The salesperson has *analyzed the causes*. S/he has discovered that the caloric intake of the individual has been steadily decreasing since the decision-maker graduated from high school. The decision-maker experienced no weight problem in high school, but has had an increasing weight problem since then. Caloric intake, the salesperson determines, is *not sufficient to cause* the problem all by itself. It is a *remote cause*; caloric intake cannot explain the recent trend toward excess weight. It is *neither a necessary* nor a *perpetuating cause*, in this case.

On the other hand, the decision-maker was always *quite active and athletic in high school*. Since graduating, s/he has taken a desk job. This has greatly reduced his/her *caloric expenditure*. The salesperson points out that this is an *immediate cause*, not a *remote cause*. It appears to have begun at about the same time the trend began. It is a *sufficient cause*; too little caloric expenditure could have caused the problem all by itself. Since the caloric intake, the other variable, has actually decreased, this could be called a *necessary cause*. By proposing the purchase and daily use of exercise equipment, the salesperson has **addressed the main cause** of the problem.

The salesperson offers *authorities, statistics, case studies*, and even a personal *anecdote* as evidence that the **proposal will work**. The salesperson shows that the exercise equipment is **affordable**; it can be paid for by eliminating some diet doctor consultations. It will be **delivered today**. The decision-maker is very **motivated** to do the exercise. Therefore, **what remains for this sale is the discussion of other problems that this proposal might help to solve**.

The salesperson can discuss the **aerobic value** of exercising on the equipment. Not only will the decision-maker lose weight, s/he will also have a *healthier heart*. The decision-maker's **good cholesterol will be increased** while his/her bad cholesterol will be reduced. His/her **respiratory system will be strengthened**. **Muscle tone** will be improved. S/he will **look younger**. S/he will **feel younger**. **Back problems** may be eliminated. **Blood pressure** will be reduced. The decision-maker will **feel more self-confident**; perhaps even **excel more** than before at work.

These are solutions to **problems that had not even been under consideration**. This is the *icing on the cake*.

In my market, I identify **three primary problems** to be solved: *medical treatment costs*, *disability needs*, and *death needs*. I complete all prior sales with regard to these problems. Now, in **Sale Number Seventeen**, I consider those **other problems that my proposal will help to solve**.

We have made certain that all of the "s-a-f-e" areas of the financial triangle are taken care of by virtue of my proposal. The decision-maker is now able to consider how best to move into the **wealth-accumulation** levels of his/her portfolio. We discuss company benefits that might be made available. The decision-maker will now be **much wiser in handling the benefits package which s/he receives**.

We talk about the **tax advantages** of the proposal that I have offered. Not only does the proposal provide for the "s-a-f-e" areas, it also does so in a strongly tax-advantaged way. I compare the tax advantages of the proposal with the tax treatment of other alternative financial instruments.

We talk about **credit life** insurance which virtually all lenders attempt to attach to credit accounts. I point out that these offers are usually over-priced. I save my clients money by showing them how to assign policy benefits instead of purchasing credit life insurance.

Choose your metaphor, "icing on the cake" or "**gravy on the steak**." It happens all the time in **Direct Marketing**. Watch a Direct Marketing commercial. After the announcer has sold you on how valuable the deals is that s/he offers you, s/he sweentes the deal. S/he offers additional freebies. Actually, the freebies are, more accurately, a **Sales Promotion element of Direct Marketing**. After selling you a GINSU knife, the announcer says "But, wait! We will also include . . .," followed by descriptions of 18 other knives and cleavers. After selling you a Ronco Pocket Fisherman or a potato slicer or a food chopper, Ron Popeil, inventor-salesperson-announcer says, "But, wait! There's more! We will also include . . .," followed by icing on the cake or gravy on the steak. Psychologically, it just helps to confirm the decision we had already determined to make that there are additional benefits to be derived from our decision that we hadn't even considered.

In **Advertising**, using a *chart to compare your product's features with those of your competitor* is called **feature analysis**. Why would companies do such a thing? The more features you offer, the higher is the likelihood that consumers might choose your product over another competitor's product (but only only if the features are **salient** [attention-drawing, standing out in a crowd] or **vivid** [relevant, important].

Whenever **high involvement** (explained in the **Introduction**) is called for, as it almost always is in **Personal Selling**, the likelihood of a **rational or informational** appeal *that emphasizes features and benefits* will succeed is increased. When **low involvement** (such as a salty snack food purchase) is appropriate, the likelihood that an **emotional appeal** will succeed is increased. Usually, **Personal Selling** is only involved in high involvement decisions. The strategy addressed in **Sale Number Seventeen** applies the psychology of *Sales Promotions* and *Direct Marketing* to the *feature analysis* of *Advertising* and produces positive results.

I have now fully explained my proposal to my decision-maker. **All that remains to be accomplished for most salespersons to consider this a real sale is the exchange of money**. This will be the conclusion of the next sale in a sale.

SALE NUMBER EIGHTEEN

You Should Enact My Proposal

Subject: Enacting my proposal.

Theme: Reasons for enacting my proposal.

Proposition: You should enact my proposal.

Interrogative: Why?

Key Word: Reasons.

Audience: Decision-maker.

Objective: To persuade the decision-maker to enact my proposal.

Divisions: (i.e., "reasons")

1. My proposal has been extremely thorough

2. My demeanor has reinforced the integrity of my proposal

3. I have offered the proposal delicately but professionally

Here is the **most delicate sale** of the twenty-one. Here is the sale that produces **cash stress** in both the *decision-maker* and the *salesperson*. Here is the sale that **results in the monetary exchange**. Without the **implicit expectation of an exchange of money**, *persuasion* is *not* termed *sales*. Yet, there have been many pieces of persuasion that have been successfully accomplished if you have even arrived at **Sale Number Eighteen**.

Some may argue that the *prior sales have been for naught unless* this sale is also accomplished. I disagree. The **ethics of selling** any product must be based upon the **belief that**

this product is good for the consumer, *whether I am paid* for selling it *or not*. If the only factor that is important to me is my paycheck, I am being very selfish, indeed.

Shortly **before my father-in-law died** suddenly of a ruptured aneurysm, he had talked to a life insurance salesperson. He was *planning on* purchasing a policy. Although the policy would *not* have been *purchased from me*, I feel certain that I influenced his decision to discuss the matter. How sorry I was that he did not get the policy in force before the day of his death. I believe in my product. I wish the other sale had been made.

I frequently talk to friends about the need for life insurance. I would never impose upon their friendship to suggest that they purchase coverage from me. Yet, *I want them to get coverage from someone*. **If a friend approaches me** about the subject, I will gladly make a proposal. I offer my advice to friends, *not to make a profit*, but because I know how the product solves problems. I consider this to be an **ethical approach**.

I am certain that **I have contributed to thousands of life insurance monetary exchange sales in addition to those for which I was paid a commission**. I have persuaded thousands regarding several of the component sales that pertain to the purchase of life insurance. *Other agents have collected the premiums and the commissions*. I still feel good about these. By the same token, I am sure that **I have completed insurance sales that others have begun**. Perhaps, I provided the sale (or two) that was missing from the other agents' presentations. I do not believe that an ethical salesperson should feel unsuccessful simply because the monetary exchange did not take place within his/her own sales process.

Having said that, however, I must admit that **it is particularly gratifying** to know that **I have solved someone's problem** and that I have also been compensated for helping. I *always try to educate* my phone prospects, prospects, decision-makers, and clients. I want them to be as *thoroughly informed* as they are willing to be about the matters that are relevant to them. I believe that **a sincere and truly informed decision-maker will generally choose to enact my proposal**. **Why** should s/he enact my proposal? There are **three reasons**.

My Proposal Has Been Extremely Thorough

Having completed all of the previous sales, I believe that **my decision-maker is in the best position s/he could possibly be in to make a decision**. If I were a presidential advisor, I would present my advice just about as thoroughly as I do for my decision-maker. I now summarize what we have accomplished, so far. I rehearse the points that have been made.

Although I may not explicitly mention it, I want to convey to my decision-maker the **first reason** *s/he should enact my proposal*: **My proposal has been extremely thorough**. Nothing that should be a matter of consideration when making a decision of this nature has been overlooked. I have referred to my recommendation as a **proposal**. This is a business term that implicitly contains a **very professional entelechy**. The several sales that have been accomplished are the very sales that a business person would need to accomplish in presenting a solid proposal to a company board of directors.

My Demeanor Has Reinforced
The Integrity of My Proposal

If the decision-maker has questions, I will **address the questions with the calmness and confidence** of a businessperson presenting a proposal. Neher, *et. al.* (1994) suggest that the "**derived *ethos***" of a communicator results *partly from **the choices of that communicator** "to use certain items of support in preference to others"* (p. 252). By citing authorities and statistics that my decision-maker considers to be reliable, I have gained derived *ethos*.

Neher, *et. al.* (1994), further claim: "Derived *ethos* is also *partly determined by **delivery**"* (p. 253). While the term delivery applies primarily to the *public speaking situation*, it also *applies in an **interpersonal sales situation***. The *entelechy* which *you as a salesperson implicitly consider to be occurring* is frequently the entelechy which the decision-maker picks up on. If you view yourself as an *aggressive, foot-in-the-door, never-take-no-for-an-answer, stereotypical salesperson*, your delivery will send that message in a hundred different ways. If you view yourself as a *businessperson presenting a business proposal to a CEO*, you will deliver your message in such a way that the **decision-maker will accept the entelechy**.

Why would I take the time to prepare a thoroughly professional proposal that commands respect only to **undercut my integrity by behaving like a pushy salesperson**? I want my decision-maker to enact my proposal for the **second** implicit **reason**: **My demeanor has reinforced the integrity of my proposal**.

I Have Offered the Proposal Delicately But Professionally

I must not change the entelechy as I arrive at the **most important sentence of the entire sales process**. I must not allow the story to be transformed from a business meeting into a sales appointment. I must *not say, "You should buy my product."*

I have **not used the term buy** or its cognate forms prior to this sale. Now is not the time to begin. When addressing my phone-prospect-turned-prospect-turned-decision-maker, I do **not typically refer to my proposal as a product**, either. The sentence must be phrased delicately. When, in my market, I have completed all of the prior sales and have reviewed and summarized my proposal, I say calmly, **"*Does this program sound like something you'd like to participate in?*"**

It is amazing how *easily a decision-maker can say yes* to this question. Once the decision-maker replies yes or I think so, I calmly take charge once again. Every message that comes from me, verbally and non-verbally, communicates **the implicit point**: "Of course, it does. That is to be completely expected."

I could have phrased the question slightly differently. *I could have said: "Does enacting my proposal make sense to you?"* Again, with a positive response, I take charge. I am now in a taking-care-of-business mode. I **calmly explain what needs to be done next**: "*There are a number of questions which I need to ask you. Some of these will not apply to you, so I have a tendency to read quickly. If one of them sounds like it might apply, let me know and I'll read it carefully for you.*" **I start right into the questions in the application**.

Eventually, I finish asking questions. I need a signature on the application. I *phrase the request delicately, yet professionally*: "***I need your signature here to certify that you have told me the truth. To the best of your knowledge and belief the answers which you have given me are true and correctly recorded.***" I *explain* the various elements of the *promissory note*, pointing out that **this is the document that defers the student's payments until s/he is out of school** and earning an income. "***I need your signature on this line. It needs to be your full signature, including your middle name.***"

I provide copies of all of the materials that we have covered to my **client** (not customer!) I tell the student that **I am very happy to have him/her as a client**. I look forward to serving him/her for a long, long time. **I mention** that our **paramedic service** will be calling within a day or two to schedule an appointment. The paramedic will come right to my client's residence. It should only take about 15 minutes. **I ask if there are any other questions**. **I tell my client** that **we have a lot of money riding on his/her life**, now. I ask him/her (kiddingly) to **be very careful when crossing the street** from now on.

Sale Number Eighteen is accomplished. I have a new client.

TWENTY-ONE SALES: PART FIVE

AUDIENCE = CLIENT

SALE NUMBER NINETEEN

You Should Accept Delivery of My Solution

Subject: Accepting delivery of my solution.

Theme: Reasons for accepting delivery of my solution.

Proposition: You should accept delivery of my solution.

Interrogative: Why?

Key Word: Reasons.

Audience: Client.

Objective: To persuade the client to accept delivery of my solution.

Divisions: (i.e., "reasons")

1. You are better qualified to be a decision-maker than anyone else you know.

2. You made an informed decision based upon very sound reasoning.

[handwritten note: - Sale complete - money recieved - doesn't always apply b/c only when time elapsed]

Now that the decision-maker has decided to become the client, **three sales typically remain**. The **first** of these sales is **not required in every instance**. Only **when time has elapsed** *between the decision to enact* the proposal *and the actual delivery of the solution* is this sale definitely required. If the solution is delivered at the time the decision is made, the salesperson may feel that this sale is irrelevant. This is not always true.

As a **consumer protection against impulse buying**, many state and federal laws and company practices exist which **allow decision-makers to change their minds**. In the insurance industry, virtually every policy includes a **10 day right to return the policy** for a full refund. I have a number of clients who hold contracts through a **company that extends this right to 20 days**. There are **cooling off periods** for *personal loans*. There are **satisfaction guarantees** offered by manufacturers, etc. Occasionally, a decision-maker experiences **buyer's remorse**, and wishes to **change his/her mind.**

When buyer's remorse occurs, even salespersons who complete delivery at the point of the decision may find that they must accomplish **Sale Number Nineteen**. Actually, while every salesperson will experience this situation occasionally, it is **not as common** as many **salespersons fear**. **Most individuals** who make a decision continue to **persuade themselves that the decision was wise.**

I remember an example of **quantitative research** that was mentioned in *a course that I took at the University of Illinois*. The participants in the study were asked to accomplish *nonsensical tasks*. The tasks were *purely arbitrary* and *no explanation was offered* to help them understand why they should do the tasks. **Those who refused** to perform the tasks were *asked later if they had made the wrong decision*. An *extremely high percentage* of them had become thoroughly persuaded that **refusal to perform** the tasks was the **wise decision**. They had developed reasoning and logic to support their decision. **Those who agreed** to perform the tasks were also *asked later if they had made the wrong decision*. An *extremely high percentage* of the members of this group also had become thoroughly persuaded that the **decision to perform** the tasks was the **wise decision**. They had developed reasoning and logic to support the decision.

Throughout the years, I have witnessed the **same phenomenon occurring in sales**. Since I am aware of it, **I also observe myself doing the same thing**. *We persuade ourselves that the decisions that we have made are the correct decisions*. I purchase a **new car** and, later **second-guess myself**. Should I have bought a less-expensive new car or a used car? **I fight back** with logic. The used car is a crap shoot. There is no guarantee against buying a lemon. With the new car, I have warranty protection. If something goes wrong, there is no additional expense. I might have bought a cheaper new car, but I will gain respect (*ethos*) by driving the more expensive one. If I purchase a used car, I justify my decision on other grounds.

Why do I thus persuade myself that whatever decision I have made is the correct one? Interpersonal communication specialists Adler and Towne (1996) cite various "[s]ocial scientists [who] have labeled this *tendency [to judge ourselves in the most generous terms possible]* the self-serving bias" (p. 111). Most of us are prone to judge ourselves and our decisions favorably. When someone suggests that we have made mistaken decisions, we tend to defend the decisions. We recount those pieces of persuasion that we have been offered that support our decisions. We invent new pieces of logic to support our decisions. Therefore, *I am hesitant to totally give up on an individual who has experienced buyer's remorse.* I believe that s/he still has the innate tendency to *defend his/her original decision.* In **Sale Number Nineteen**, I present two reasons for accepting the delivery of my solution. Reason number one is the following reminder to my client:

You are Better Qualified to Be a Decision-Maker Than Anyone Else You Know

I have discovered that a **client who second-guesses** a decision **has usually been criticized** or embarrassed by someone else whom s/he considers to be credible. Perhaps, a *spouse* or a *parent* has reacted unfavorably toward the decision. Individuals who are prone to having *low self-esteem are very susceptible* to the unfavorable reaction of others. The **criticism** which others have offered is **almost invariably based upon a misunderstanding** of some part of the transaction.

I truly believe that **any individual who has completed the sales process with me is much more knowledgeable about the details of the transaction than anyone who is criticizing** the client. My **client is the one who is best qualified** to be a decision-maker. At times, the client *simply needs to hear this.* If someone has criticized the decision, I **invite that critic to be present** at delivery. I **may need to make the critic into an informed decision-maker.** If the critic cannot come, I **encourage the client to ask the critic for specific questions** that must be answered. In other words, **I want my client to claim what is rightfully his/hers--respect.** S/he has not made an unintelligent or an uninformed decision. S/he should not let others imply that s/he has.

You Made an Informed Decision
Based Upon Very Sound Reasoning

This is the **second reason** that I provide to my client for accepting the delivery of my solution. Depending upon the attitude that my client displays when we get together for delivery, I may **provide a very thorough or a very brief review of the information that prompted the decision.** The key point is that my client has **probably already forgotten** some of the information. This simply **reinforces the contention** that I made in **Sale Number Thirteen**: *You will be more knowledgeable about this issue and this proposal, when I finish, than ever before and probably ever again.* I want my client to remember one thing: **S/he was very informed** when his/her decision was made. If the client **needs to have his/her memory refreshed** on any specific portion of the proposal, I offer him/her an opportunity to request such further information. As I review the information that I provided in previous sales, **I demonstrate in the client's solution (the product) where such information is found and how such information is utilized.**

I remind my client that **I am available should any questions arise** regarding this solution. I encourage my client to **always call me first** with questions. Then, **I ask my client to sign that s/he has received** the materials.

Among the **Four P's of marketing**, we have emphasized the **Product** (in **Sale Number Two**), the **Price** (in **Sale Number Sixteen**), and the **Promotions** (meaning in the "marketing" sense, all "marketing communication," in virtually **every Sale**). In **Sale Number Nineteen**, we emphasize the **Place** (or *distribution* or *delivery system*). **Personal selling** (unlike retail sales) **does not** typically **require the purchaser to come to the salesperson's Place** of business, in order to complete the transaction. Instead, the salesperson **may deliver** the product *in person* or *by mail* or using *some other form of shipping*. The **advantage** of this concept of **Place** in marketing is that *it is unnecessary to provide a huge retail or office area* in which to transact business. The **disadvantage** is that *time frequently elapses between purchase and delivery.* The **psychological phenomenon** (discussed in **Sale Number Nineteen**) seen in the University of Illinois research is **not as reliable** when there seems to be **some level of incompleteness in the transaction.** Although we typically will justify to ourselves whatever decisions we have made, if we sense that we have not "finally" decided anything until we take delivery, this justification phenomenon may actually work against the completion of the purchase. For example, I have had agents who marketed insurance on the premise that, since there is a 10 day right to return the policy, the prospect does not need to decide today—s/he can wait until the policy comes in. This approach is disasterous. The delivery sale is not to take the place the deciding sale (where the exchange of money is transacted). That sale was made in Sale Number Eighteen. Some reselling may be necessary at delivery, however, if it has not been made very clear to the client that the transaction is complete by the end of Sale Number Eighteen.

SALE NUMBER TWENTY

You Should Continue to Be My Client

Subject: Continuing to be my client.

Theme: Reasons for continuing to be my client.

Proposition: You should continue to be my client.

Interrogative: Why?

Key Word: Reasons.

Audience: Client.

Objective: To persuade the client to continue to be my client.

Divisions: (i.e., "reasons")

1. I promise to serve you honestly and competently

2. You have invested in my services

3. I have subsequent *ethos*

With the completion of **Sale Number Nineteen**, much of the tension that you are experiencing as a salesperson will be relieved. You may feel inclined to leave before the client changes his/her mind. However, this is a **perfect time to reinforce your *ethos***. There may be **many future business transactions** with this *client*. There may be future business transactions with the *client's friends and associates*. This business transaction is now complete, so it is time to relax, smile, and **show goodwill**. **It has taken nineteen sales to gain a client. It may only take one sale to keep that client.** Why not make that sale?

The **three reasons my client should remain my client** are as follows:

I Promise to Serve You
Honestly and Competently

Now that my first proposal has been enacted and the solution delivered, I want to remind my client that **when s/he first listened** to the audio recording I provided, s/he heard me list my **credentials as a competent professional.** I express **hope** that throughout our business transaction **s/he has found me to be competent**. I mention that *competence* in my profession *requires me to continue to keep abreast of the latest laws, strategies, and ratings of companies.* I want my client to be able to relax, knowing that *s/he will always be able to call on a professional in this field* whom s/he knows. I *provide my telephone number* again.

I also remind my client that, on the recording, **I promised not to treat anyone in a way that I would not appreciate being treated myself.** I now reiterate that *I mean that.* If, as my client, the individual ever desires more help than I have provided, I want to know. If s/he needs financial services that I am not licensed to provide, *I will gladly recommend other professionals.* In short, I am asking the client to let me know if there is anything that I can do to improve the level of service. I state that I have always been *honest with my client.* I ask my client to always *be honest with me.*

You Have Invested in My Services

I point out that my client has invested in my services. To fail to contact me, if a problem or a question arises, is to **fail to achieve the full value** of the program that we have established. Since my service is in the area of financial planning, I strongly advise my clients to make full use of their investments. **I am one of their investments.** They should make full use of my services.

210

I Have Subsequent *Ethos*

Neher, *et. al.* (1994) define **"subsequent *ethos*"** as the *ethos* that is "determined by events that occur after the end [of the communication encounter] . . . the sum of both initial and derived *ethos*" (p. 253). For example, *if someone has seriously criticized my proposal* to my client, I have **lost** *ethos*. *If someone has praised me or my proposal* to my client, I have **gained** *ethos*. The very fact that I have the confidence to deliver the product and to refrain from rushing off once delivery is complete helps to further establish my *ethos*. While my prospect may not have paid attention to anything concerning my **reputation** prior to our transaction, s/he will now listen to any comments that reflect upon my reputation. Indeed, the client will now contribute either **positively** or **negatively** to my reputation. Every client that you gain is a letter of recommendation. It is absolutely essential that you have many clients providing positive **subsequent *ethos***. They represent and influence the future of your business.

In **Public Relations**, one of **the "publics"** (referred to as "stakeholders" in IMC) **with whom we try to develop good relations** is **Customers** (or, in the entelechy I recommend, **Clients**). Other publics are: *employees, government regulators, competitors, consumer groups*, etc. Clearly, **client relations** (customer relations) is an **important facet** of Public Relations. It is important to keep clients/customers happy after the sale. An IMC concept, **Relationship Marketing**, which is closely related to Public Relations, pertains to all the stakeholders of the company—those "publics" mentioned above, plus *distributors, channel members, agencies, investors, media*, and the *community*. **Customer Relationship Management** is a variation of Relationship Marketing that originates in **Sales Management** utilizing **databases** to direct communication with customers.

In **Advertising**, brand loyalty often occurs when a personal experience develops into a relationship over time. **Loyalty programs** (like the airlines' frequent flyer programs) cross the lines between **Sales Promotions** (since they offer incentives to have repeat business), **Advertising** (since these programs are definitely advertised), and **Public Relations** (since they cultivate strong relationships with their customers).

SALE NUMBER TWENTY-ONE

You Should Provide a Reference for Me

Subject: Providing a reference for me.

Theme: Reasons for providing a reference for me.

Proposition: You should provide a reference for me.

Interrogative: Why?

Key Word: Reasons.

Audience: Client.

Objective: To persuade the client to provide a reference for me.

Divisions: (i.e., "reasons")

> 1. The business entelechy
>
> 2. The help I have supplied

The **final sale** is here. There was a *monetary transaction* in **Sale Number Eighteen**. Clearly, that could be termed a sale. There was a *delivery of your side of the contract* in **Sale Number Nineteen**. Although the money exchanged hands earlier, it is easy to see that implicitly this sale was linked to the monetary transaction. In **Sale Number Twenty**, there is the hope of future monetary transactions, so long as *the individual remains your client*. But, **why** would I call the **request for a reference** a sale? *College students ask their professors* to provide references. These are not sales. *Church members ask their ministers* to provide references. These are not sales. *Employees ask their employers* to provide references. These are not sales. *Friends ask friends* to provide references. These are not sales.

The Business Entelechy

I agree. Asking for a reference usually is not interpreted as a sale. This is the **precise reason that asking for a "reference" makes such a good sale!** Throughout *Making offers they can't refuse*, I have presented the sales process in **business terminology**. I have recommended that the *phone prospect* be referred to by *terms of respect*. I have recommended the *use of "Mr." or "Ms." or "Dr." when referring to oneself*. I have recommended *professional courtesy* when using the telephone. I have recommended emphasizing *one's professional expertise*. I have recommended *forewarning of the expectation of a decision*.

When you make the presentation to the decision-maker, I have recommended incorporating *all of the component parts of a thorough business proposal*. I even *refer to my offer as a proposal*. Indeed, you may well use the information in this book to supplement a good text on making business proposals, such as Bud Porter-Roth's book, *Proposal development: How to respond and win the bid* (1998). I recommend *using causal analysis, feasibility and workability studies*, as well as references to *other incidental problems that will be solved* by enacting your proposal.

The *very reason you request a* **reference** *is that this terminology is not sales terminology*. If, at the very end of a sales presentation, you ask for **sales "referrals," you destroy the entelechy** that you have labored throughout the sales process to create. Everyone has been asked for *referrals*. This **request is interpreted as** the request: **"Will you now sick me on your friends?"** You should work diligently to **avoid this entelechy**.

Since your *client is a business acquaintance*, it is **perfectly normal to ask for permission** to use the client's name as *a reference*, or *even to ask the client for a brief letter of reference*. It is far better to be able to use the name of an individual who will provide **positive subsequent** *ethos* than to dig out the names of referrals. These unwillingly rendered referrals will often hear a tone of *resentment* in the voice of my client when they mention that you called them.

The Help I Have Supplied

What type of reference do you desire? **Only ask the client to consider whether or not you have been helpful.** This request alone is tantamount to asking the client to praise you to others. You *might violate rules of modesty* by either *claiming that you have helped* or by *suggesting ways that you may have helped.* There is a delicate balance between providing *ethos* for yourself and bragging. Yet you know that you have helped the client solve some problems. You may not know what part of your proposal was most important to the client. By **asking the client to consider whether or not you have been helpful**, the client may be able to further solidify the relationship. S/he leaves the sales process considering the ways in which s/he has been helped. This is a *great way to conclude the process.*

In **Sale Number Nine**, we considered how the **Diffusion of Innovations** as a form of Marketing Communication might be used to consider whether a new technology was ready yet to be used in your marketing efforts. We identified five levels of diffusion:

- **innovators** (those who are among the first to try new technologies and products),
- **early adopters** (those who are willing to try the innovations after innovators have tested them),
- **early majority** (the first major influx of many new users)
- **late majority** (the second major influx of many new users)
- **laggards** (those who are the last to try new technologies and products)

In **Sale Number Twenty-One**, we consider how word-of-mouth applies to your sales. **Your product and services** are now the **"innovation." Your new client** may be an **innovator** (one of the first in your market to invest in your proposal) or s/he may be a **laggard** (one of the later individuals to invest) or s/he may be somewhere in the middle (**early adopter, early majority,** or **late majority**). Wherever s/he is on the continuum, you will notice that s/he can help to persuade others to try your innovation. Even laggards influence other laggards. **Once you have begun to develop early and late majorities** who are willing to try your product or service, you will find this list of references you are developing to be an important **database value,** as the **herd mentality** mentioned in **Sale Number Nine** begins to operate **positively** for you.

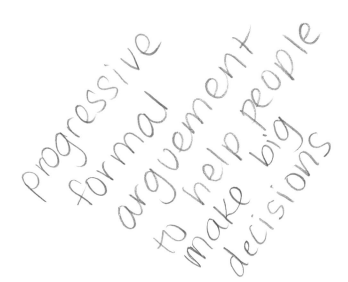

CONCLUSION

Syllogistic Progressive Form

Personal Selling, as type of marketing communication, differs significantly from most **Retail Selling**. Although the retail salesperson is called a "salesperson," most of his/her **selling has already been done for him/her.** It was **not as important** for the retail salesperson **to sell himself or herself** that *there is a need for the product* or that *the product is a proper solution* for the problem. Various **business-to-business (B2B)** Marketing Communication departments of the **product brand** have already accomplished much of this by **selling the wholesaler and retailer on the need to carry the product (channel marketing).** **Retailers** have already responded positively by deciding to carry the product. Although the **retail salesperson may have needed to sell himself or herself** that *s/he was the right person to sell this solution*, s/he typically **did not need** to **sell himself or herself** *to do market research* or *to call prospects.* **Brand Advertising** and **Retail Advertising** completed several sales for the Retail salesperson:

- *You should give me a minute of your time.*
- *This matter is relevant to you.*

- *We are a legitimate enterprise.*
- *It is worthwhile for you to consider more information on this subject.*
- *You have a problem.*
- *Our proposal addresses the cause of your problem.*
- *Our proposal will work to solve your problem.*
- *Our proposal is feasible.*
- *Our proposal will help to solve other problems.*

The retail salesperson **may not even need** to complete the sale that *s/he is well-qualified to help you*. I'm **not even certain** that the retail salesperson needs to persuade the prospect that *s/he should enact the proposal*. The prospect may have already done self-persuasion in that area, as well. Frequently, the retail salesperson is just a **facilitator**, *helping the customer complete the purchase.*

What Aristotle called a **chain of syllogisms**, Kenneth Burke (1968) called **syllogistic progressive form** (p. 124-127). *Syllogistic progressive form* simply suggests logic in the development of any persuasive message. The *major premise* and at least one *minor premise* must be established as credible with the audience before *conclusions* can be drawn. Then, in turn, these newly established *conclusions* may be employed as *premises* for *other conclusions*, until one reaches the **final conclusion**, the point that the persuader is ultimately attempting to persuade his/her audience to accept. "In so far as the audience, from its acquaintance with the premises, feels the rightness of the conclusion, the work is **formal** [meaning that it has syllogistic progressive **form**]" (CS 124). In *Making offers they can't refuse*, we have used **progressive form**. **Sale Number Two** could not be accomplished until **Sale Number One** had been completed, *and so on, and so on*, until we reached **Sale Number Twenty-One**.

In **Part One**, you began with the most honest and ethical of sales, the five sales to **yourself** (the *intra*personal sales). You persuaded **yourself** that *there is a need for your product. A problem exists.* Only then, could you persuade **yourself** that *your product is a proper solution for the need/problem.* After that, you needed to persuade **yourself** that *you are the right person to sell this solution*, and only if that is the case, that *you should do market research* and, after you do the research, that *you should call your prospects.*

When you are ready to call your **phone prospects**, you move to **Part Two**, the first *inter*personal contact. The entire group of four sales takes only one minute to accomplish, but before you could make the final three sales, you had to persuade your **phone prospect** to *give you just one minute of time*. Responsibly and courteously, you ask for only one minute of time. Once the minute is granted, you quickly establish for your **phone prospect** the *relevance of the subject* and present the *legitimacy of your business entity* for dealing with the subject. You hope that this one minute conversation will finally persuade the phone prospect that *it is worthwhile for him/her to consider more information on the subject.*

In **Part Three**, the phone prospect has become a legitimate **prospect**. S/he has expressed some level of interest in receiving information on the topic, so you may now—but not before— give the additional information and make the sales in that information. The **first three of the four sales** that are made to the prospect at this stage may be accomplished by **technological** means. You need to persuade the **prospect** that *s/he has a problem*. The **prospect** must be persuaded that *you and your business entity are well qualified to help* the prospect and that *you have a proposal for helping the prospect that is worth considering.*

The final sale of **Part Three** must be made **in person**. Much has been said about the importance of *treating the prospect ethically*. Here, not only do you treat the prospect ethically, but also the ***prospect learns to treat you ethically***. You persuade the **prospect** that *s/he should agree to become a decision-maker.*

In **Part Four**, the prospect has become a **decision-maker**. You cannot get the cart before the horse; you must wait until the prospect becomes a decision-maker to present your proposal. The five sales in this part comprise nothing less than a **legitimate business proposal**. You are inducing the **decision-maker** to become your *client*, not customer. You employ ***causal analysis*** to persuade the **decision-maker** that *your proposal addresses the cause of the problem*. You provide statistics, case studies, and anecdotal evidence to persuade the **decision-maker** that *your proposal works*. You address the four ***feasibility*** issues, persuading the **decision-maker** that *your proposal is feasible*. You persuade the **decision-maker** that *the proposal may also help to solve other incidental problems*. This is a thorough proposal. Upon completion, you--the professional--recommend to the **decision-maker**: *"You should enact my proposal."* **Now, the**

decision-maker has a *choice.* **Only if the choice is "yes,"** will the **decision-maker** become your **client**.

In **Part Five, three final sales** remain to be made to **your client**. 1) The *solution* (i.e., product) must be *delivered.* 2) The long-term professional-**client** *relationship must be solidified.* 3) The **client** must be asked for a *reference.* Clearly, you must not ask for a reference, unless you have established a relationship with your **client**, and you cannot establish a relationship until the product is delivered. With these final three sales completed, your syllogistic chain/**syllogistic progressive form** is complete. You have been completely thorough in your presentation. Congratulations! **You have made an offer they couldn't refuse!**

REFERENCES

Adler, R. B. and Towne, N. (1996). *Looking out/looking in: Interpersonal communication* (8th ed.). Fort Worth, TX: Harcourt Brace College Publishers.

Aristotle (1991). *Aristotle on rhetoric: A theory of civic discourse*. G. A. Kennedy (Trans.). New York & Oxford: Oxford University Press.

Astrachan, J. B. (1988, May 23). When to name a competitor. *Adweek*.

Axelrod, R. B. and Cooper, C. R. (1994). *The St. Martin's guide to writing* (4th ed., short ed.). New York: St. Martin's Press.

Baron, G.R. (1997). *Friendship marketing: Growing your business by cultivating strategic relationships.* Grants Pass, OR: Oasis Press/PSI Research.

Berko, R. M., Rosenfeld, L. B., and Samovar, L. A. (1997). *Connecting: A culture-sensitive approach to interpersonal communication competency* (2nd ed.) Ft. Worth, TX: Harcourt Brace College Publishers.

Bovee, C. L. and Thill, J. V. (1995). *Business communication today*, (4th ed.). New York: McGraw-Hill.

Burke, Kenneth. (1943). The five master terms: Their place in a "dramatistic" grammar of motives. *View* 3 (2), 50-52.

---. (1966). *Language as symbolic action: Essays on life, literature, and method*. Berkeley: University of California Press.

---. (1968). *Counter-statement*. Berkeley: University of California Press.

---. (1969). *A grammar of motives*. Berkeley: University of California Press.

---. (1970). Poetics and communication. In H. E Kiefer and M. K. Munitz (Eds.), *Perspectives in education, religion, and the arts* 401-418. Albany: State University of New York Press.

---. (1972). *Dramatism and development*. Barre, MA: Clark University Press with Barre Publishers.

Copley, P. (2004). *Marketing communications management: Concepts and theories, cases and practices*. Amsterdam: Butterworth Heinemann.

Davis, D. A. (1996). *Develop and market your creative ideas*. Grants Pass, OR: Oasis Press/PSI Research.

Drescher, N. (1997). *Which business? Help in selecting your new venture*. Grants Pass, OR: Oasis Press/PSI Research.

Frigstad, D. B. (1994). *Know your market: How to do low-cost market research.* Grants Pass, OR: Oasis Press/PSI Research.

Jannach, H. (1961). *German for reading knowledge.* New York: American Book Company.

Klausner, S. Z. (Ed.). (1968). *Why man takes chances: Studies in stress-seeking.* Garden City, NY: Doubleday.

Lindsay, S. A. (1998a). *Implicit rhetoric: Kenneth Burke's extension of Aristotle's concept of entelechy.* Lanham, MD: University Press of America.

---. (1998b). *The twenty-one sales in a sale: What sales are you missing?* Grants Pass, OR: Oasis Press/PSI Research.

---. (2004a). *Persuasion, proposals, and public speaking.* Orlando: Say Press.

---. (2004b). *The seven Cs of stress: A Burkean approach.* Orlando: Say Press, 2004.

---. (2005), *Psychotic entelechy: The dangers of "spiritual gift" theology.* Lanham, MD: University Press of America.

---. (2009). *Persuasion, proposals, and public speaking* (2nd ed.). Orlando: Say Press.

McKeon, R. (1973). *Introduction to Aristotle* (2nd ed.). Chicago and London: University of Chicago Press.

Neher, W. W., Waite, D. H., Cripe, N., and Flood, R. E. (1994). *Public speaking: A rhetorical approach* (3rd ed.). Dubuque, IA: Kendall/Hunt.

Newberg, J. and Marcus, C. (1996). *TargetSmart! Database marketing for the small business.* Grants Pass, OR: Oasis Press/PSI Research.

O'Hair, D., Friedrich, G. W., Wiemann, J. M., and Wiemann, M. O. (1997). *Competent communication* (2nd ed.). New York: St. Martin's Press.

Plato (1968). *The republic.* B. Jowett (Trans.). New York: Airmont.

Plato (1971). *Gorgias.* W. Hamilton (Trans.). London: Penguin.

Plato (1973). *Phaedrus and the seventh and eighth letters,* W. Hamilton (Trans.). London: Penguin.

Porter-Roth, B. (1998). *Proposal development: How to respond and win the bid.* Grants Pass, OR: Oasis Press/PSI Research.

Rogers, E. M. (1995). *Diffusion of innovations* (4th ed.). New York: The Free Press.

Schiappa, E. (1992). *Rhetorikē*: What's in a name? Toward a revised history of early Greek rhetorical theory. *Quarterly Journal of Speech*, 78, 1-15.

Smith, R. E. (1995). *Principles of human communication* (4th ed.). Dubuque, IA: Kendall/Hunt.

Sprague, J. and Stuart, D. (2000). *The speaker's handbook* (5th ed.) Fort Worth: Harcourt College Publishers.

Toulmin, S. E. (1964). *The uses of argument.* London: Cambridge University Press.

Trenholm, S. and Jensen, A. (1992). *Interpersonal communication* (2nd ed.). Belmont, CA: Wadsworth.

Weaver, R. M. (1953). *The ethics of rhetoric*. South Bend, IN: Henry Regnery.

INDEX

Made in the USA
Charleston, SC
02 January 2015